Adoption by foster carers

A guide to preparing, assessing and supporting foster carers adopting children in their care

Elaine Dibben and Viv Howorth

Published by
CoramBAAF Adoption and Fostering Academy
41 Brunswick Square
London WC1N 1AZ
www.corambaaf.org.uk

Coram Academy Limited, registered as a company limited by guarantee
in England and Wales number 9697712, part of the Coram group, charity
number 312278

© CoramBAAF, 2016

British Library Cataloguing in Publication Data
A catalogue record for this book is available from the British Library

ISBN 978 1 910039 44 1

Project management by Jo Francis, Publications Department,
CoramBAAF
Designed and typeset by Helen Joubert Design
Printed in Great Britain by The Lavenham Press

Contents

Acknowledgements

We are very grateful to the foster carer adopters who responded to our request to contact us about their experiences – particularly those who then took the time to document their stories for us. These accounts really help to capture the nature of the relationships and attachments that are such a key feature of foster carer adoptions and provide a better understanding of how adoption agency processes impacted on them and their families.

We would like to thank social work colleagues who responded to requests to provide information about their existing policies, and in particular Judith Matthews, Margaret Orchard, Teresa Vickers, Sarah Carter and Dawn May, who took the time to meet and/or talk to us in more depth about practice in their agency and to comment on this book. We would also like to thank Wendy Keiden, Priscilla McLoughlin and Barbara Hudson and their colleagues for their assistance in providing information about foster carers adopting in Wales, Northern Ireland and Scotland. Thanks also to Paul Adams who provided us with feedback on the script.

We are grateful to Sheffield City Council Family Placement Services for allowing us to use some recent case material.

We would also like to thank Shaila Shah and Jo Francis in CoramBAAF Publications, who have stuck with us over the rather prolonged period of writing this book and offered their wisdom and a keen eye to bring it together as a final document.

Notes about the authors

Elaine Dibben started her social work career in residential social work and qualified in 1988. She has over 25 years' experience of working in adoption and fostering in local authority and voluntary adoption agency settings. She joined BAAF in 2004 to become manager of the Independent Review Mechanism, which she set up and ran until 2009, when she moved to take on a wider role in BAAF as a trainer/consultant. She is currently an Adoption Development Consultant for CoramBAAF, alongside acting as a Panel Chair for both adoption and fostering panels.

She was part of the DfE Expert Working Party on adoption, set up in 2012 to inform adoption policy, and currently sits on the National Recruitment Forum, a sub-group of the Adoption Leadership Board. She has written several books, published by BAAF – *Devising a Placement Plan* (2012), *Parent and Child Fostering*, with Paul Adams (2011), *Preparing to Adopt* (2014), with Eileen Fursland and Nicky Probert, *Undertaking an Adoption Assessment in England* (2010) (second edition 2013), and *Completing a Child's Permanence Report* (2014).

Elaine and Viv co-authored a guide on foster carers wishing to make the transition to adoption for the Community Care Inform website in April 2012 which started them thinking about writing this Good Practice Guide. She lives in Oxfordshire with her husband, Steve.

Viv Howorth commenced her social work career in residential settings in the North West of England and then continued her professional career as a qualified worker in South Yorkshire. She has 30 years' experience of working in children and families teams and fostering and adoption work. In 2004, Viv joined BAAF as a trainer consultant in Yorkshire and Humber and was BAAF Northern Regional Director between 2012 and 2014, when she worked with Elaine on the above-mentioned guide on foster carers wishing to make the transition to adoption for the Community Care Inform website. Viv has now returned to social work practice as a part-time adoption social worker and is also continuing independent work such as chairing adoption and fostering panels and some training. Viv lives in South Yorkshire.

Introduction

In recent years, there has been increased Government and media focus on the benefits of adoption for children in care who cannot return to their birth families, the importance of reducing the time children wait for a permanent placement, and the need to increase the number of adoptive families available. This is now a pertinent time to look in more detail at the potential resource being offered by foster carers wanting to adopt children in their care and to ensure that there is a shared understanding of the potential benefits and challenges in making these adoptive placements.

In writing this Good Practice Guide, we recognise that every case is different, so that whilst we set out our view of what needs to be considered in the decision making around foster carers adopting children in their care, we would suggest that ultimately each case must be decided on its individual merits, recognising that there may well be a balancing exercise around strengths, concerns and areas needing support.

We primarily focus on foster carer adoptions within the context of the legislative framework in England and Wales, but the issues discussed in this guide apply to all of the countries in the UK.

Whilst adoption by foster carers has always been possible, it is an area of adoption practice that has attracted divergent views and controversy over the last 30 years. Controversial cases have been featured in local or national press stories or have found their way into contested proceedings, which can be stressful for all involved. Differencs have been voiced within and between teams about the advantages and disadvantages of making such placements.

In this Good Practice Guide, we explore some of the issues behind the contradictory views and perceived challenges. We have also talked to agencies and professionals who responded to our requests to hear about agencies' experiences, and share some examples of their practice and some of the forms and policies that they have developed and which have helped them in this area. We hope that by sharing practice from different agencies and reflecting on experiences of foster carers who have adopted, we can establish how this route to adoption can be maximised for those children and foster carers for whom adoption is the right plan.

In preparation for this guide, foster carers were invited to contact us about their experiences, resulting in a number of responses. Fourteen carers followed this initial contact with a written account of their experiences, including two who provided a response through their social worker (FCA 10 and FCA 11). Their personal accounts provide evidence of successful placements of the children they adopted and demonstrate the depth of emotions that they experienced through the adoption process. Their experiences are vividly illustrated in their own words (under coded names), and summaries of their situations are given in Appendix 1 to provide further context.

> We have adopted three children who we were fostering in our 35 years as carers. Our first is now 19 and achieved 10 passes at GCSE and is now at college.
> FCA 9

> It was R's wish to be adopted by our family…He adopted us in many ways.
> FCA 13

TERMINOLOGY AND REMIT OF THIS GUIDE

There is no specific terminology used in legislation for foster carers who adopt, but for clarity in this guide we use the term "carer adopter" when referring to a foster carer who is considering or is in the process of adopting a child in their care.

It is worth briefly mentioning Fostering for Adoption (FFA) and dual-approval schemes, as these are not covered in this Good Practice Guide. In the last couple of years, the renewed interest in concurrent planning and the introduction of FFA into legislation in the Children and Families Act 2014 has caused some confusion in the minds of the public and some professionals about the role of FFA placements and foster carers adopting children in their care. FFA is a type of early permanence in which approved prospective adopters are also approved as foster carers for a specific child so that the child can be placed with them before the child's plan for adoption has been agreed by the courts and a placement order made. If a placement order is made, the placement can then become an adoption placement.

The Department for Education (DfE) notes in Statutory Guidance (2014b) that:

> The advantage of this type of placement (FFA) is that the child will be placed with foster carers who, subject to a placement order being made, or parental consent, are expected to go on to become the child's adoptive family. Delay in finding a permanent family for young children who have already experienced neglect early on in their lives may have a profoundly damaging effect on their development. This type of placement has potential to reduce this delay and the damage caused significantly.

It is interesting to note that the recognised benefits of minimising delay and reducing placement moves can also equally be applied to those situations where a short-term foster carer adopts a child, but the difference in the status of the carer and the way in which the plan is made means that a much more varied response is experienced.

Further information about FFA can be found in the Fostering for Adoption Practice Guidance published by BAAF and Coram (2013) and in Borthwick and Donnelly's guide to concurrent planning (2013).

Specific projects have also been set up to encourage foster carers to consider how they can offer permanence to a child in their care, such as schemes where prospective carers are dually approved as foster carers and adopters and are matched with a child for whom they will provide a permanent placement. The children are placed under fostering regulations, but the carers work towards offering adoption or special guardianship to that child within three years. This is a model that some voluntary adoption agencies and local authorities are exploring.

While there may be some practice similarities between these types of schemes and foster carers adopting a child in their care, this Good Practice Guide does not consider FFA or dual-approval schemes.

Chapter 1
Research findings on foster carer adoption

In recent years, there has been a small increase in the number of foster carers adopting children in their care, which we refer to as carer adoption. However, statistics show that there is variation in the practice of adoption by foster carers in the four countries of the UK and across different local authorities.

EARLIER FINDINGS ON FOSTER CARER ADOPTION

In 2000, Ivaldi reported that foster carers accounted for 13 per cent of all adoptions. He found that, on average, children being adopted by their foster carers were almost twice as old at entry into care and two years older than other children in the research sample, with the average age being six years and three months. He also noted that carer adopters were older than the average (with over 42 per cent being over 45 years old) and represented nearly half of the single carers in the study. He further noted that 27 per cent of the mixed heritage children adopted transracially in the study were adopted by their foster carers, and had been the longest in care before a decision for adoption was made. In his study, 40 per cent of the adopting foster carers had identified that they would need an adoption allowance.

Ivaldi compared the percentage of foster carers adopting in the UK with the number of children adopted by their foster carers in the USA, which in 1998 was 65 per cent of all adoptions from care, with most of these families being granted 'substantial allowances which only fall slightly short of foster care allowances' (2000, p111).

Ivaldi recommended that further policy work was urgently needed to look at 'how foster carer applications to adopt should be viewed and whether they should be actively encouraged where the child has a strong attachment' (p112). He felt that there would be 'considerable potential benefits...for many children if they could have a permanent legal status with their carer which would recognise the life-long commitment made by the new families' (p112).

Although there has been some further research from Biehal *et al* in 2010, there has been little evidence of any significant policy work being taken forward in this area.

FOSTER CARER ADOPTION IN THE USA

The most recent statistics from the USA, from October 2013, show that 50,608 children were adopted, with 30 per cent being adopted by relatives (with 20 per cent of those being related foster carers), 53 per cent by non-related foster carers and 17 per cent by non-related adopters.

There has been a significant change in attitudes to foster carer adoptions in the USA. In the 1970s, a distinction was made between foster carers – who were seen as only offering temporary care – and adopters – where there was a specific matching process for the children placed with them. However, by the early 1980s, there was recognition from permanency planning projects of the benefits of foster carer adoption. The Federal Adoption Assistance and Child Welfare Act of 1980 (P.L. 96-272) supported foster carer adoption by introducing financial subsidies for children adopted from foster care (Proch, 1981). Practice changed gradually over time and foster carers are now recognised as a valuable resource for waiting children, with 28 States providing procedures for foster carers to adopt when their foster child becomes legally free for adoption.

In January 2013, the Child Welfare Information Gateway published *A Guide to Preparing and Supporting Foster Parents who Adopt*. This guide sets out the recognised benefits of foster carer adoption, as follows:

- *Research indicates that children waiting for adoption by their foster carers are less likely to experience disruption than children in non-relative, non-foster-parent adoption (Berry and Barth, 1990; McRoy, 1999; Smith and Howard, 1991)*

- *A continuing and legally secure relationship with foster carers they know and trust*

- *An end to the uncertainty of foster care and, for many children, a positive psychological shift in their sense of identity, connection, and belonging (Triseliotis, 2003)*

- *The chance to remain in a familiar community, school, and neighbourhood*

- *Tendency for shorter time to permanency than in other types of adoption (Howard and Smith, 2003)*

- *Greater likelihood of maintaining an ongoing connection with the birth family than in families formed through matching (Howard and Smith, 2003)*

- *Experienced parents to manage their needs (often including emotional and behavioral challenges due to trauma and complicated life histories)*

- *An established legal permanency for children and youth who would otherwise be wards of the court*

It also recognised potential benefits for a child's birth family:

- *Foster carer adoption sometimes means that the birth parents know and can have a relationship with those who will be the permanent caregivers for their children.*

- *Foster carer adoptions are often open – an adoption arrangement in which identities are known and there is direct contact between birth families and adoptive families – either because a relationship developed between the birth and adoptive parents when the children were in care or because the children know their birth families' contact information and may contact them after adoption. More than one-third of all children who have been adopted (36 per cent) had some post-adoption contact with their birth families (Vandivere et al, 2009).*

Whilst accepting that there are cultural and legislative differences, it is worth considering whether social workers and policy-makers could become more open and positive to foster carer adoption, with the potential of leading to an increase in placements, as seen in the USA.

THE CURRENT SITUATION IN ENGLAND

In England, Government statistics show that over the last few years there has been an incremental increase in the number of children being adopted by their foster carers, rising from 360 children in 2009/10 to 750 children in 2013/14. The proportion of children adopted by their foster carers each year has increased slightly in the last two years, from 11–12 per cent to 15 per cent of all children adopted.

However, statistics on children *placed* for adoption with their foster carers, which had been showing a small but gradual increase (from 260 children in 2009/10 (10%) to 500 children in 2013/14 (13%)), then showed a drop in numbers to 350 children in 2014/15 (11%), which may impact on future adoption figures.

There are no nationwide statistics on the proportion of foster carers adopting, categorised by local authority. In our discussions with some local authorities, we were able to obtain their local data, including some information about the children achieving permanence through carer adoption – these data may be helpful for other agencies to use as comparators when examining their own statistics. The local authorities cited below have been proactive in setting up procedures for foster carers wanting to adopt children in their care and have seen some increases in their numbers as a result.

Local Authority 1 placed 170 children for adoption in 2013/14. A total of 25 of these children (15%) were adopted by their foster carer/family. This included three sibling groups of two, and six children who were aged five or over; three of the 25 children had a disability. It can be seen from these figures that over half of these children would generally be considered "harder to place".

Local Authority 2 placed 116 children for adoption in 2013/14, and approved 15 foster carer households to adopt children in their care, with four of those families adopting more than one child. Therefore, 16 per cent of the local authority's children were adopted by their foster carers. This was a significant increase from seven foster carer households approved to adopt in 2012/13, which had represented only 6.5 per cent of the children adopted.

Local Authority 3 had 64 children adopted in 2014/15. Six of these children were adopted by their foster carers, accounting for nearly 10 per cent. Five of the six children were aged five or over and this included a sibling group of two, aged 7 and 10 at the time. One of the children adopted by foster carers had a significant disability (chronic lung disease) and another had speech and language difficulties and displayed hard to manage behaviour, requiring additional support. At the time of writing in 2015/16, three children had been adopted by their foster carers, accounting for over 10 per cent. One of these children was aged 11 at the time of adoption and their plan had previously changed from adoption to long-term fostering. Another was aged five at the time of adoption and had returned to their foster carer following a disruption in an adoptive placement. There were a further nine children who were in the process of being adopted by their foster carers, six of whom were over the age of five, including a 15-year-old whose placement order had previously been revoked, a sibling group of three where the original plan was for one child to be long-term fostered (they are now all being adopted together), and a two-year-old who had been returned to their original foster carers following a disrupted adoptive placement and was now being adopted by them.

THE CURRENT SITUATION IN WALES, SCOTLAND AND NORTHERN IRELAND

In **Wales**, 385 children were adopted from care during the year ending 31 March 2014, with 40 adopted by their foster carer. Although this accounts for a significant 10 per cent of adoptions, there has been little focus on carer adoptions in adoption policy.

In **Scotland**, there are no figures collected on foster carer adoptions, so it is not possible to comment on the overall picture, although the legislative guidance is set out later in this chapter.

In **Northern Ireland**, a high proportion of children who are adopted are adopted by their foster carers. However, the majority of these carers are dually approved as adopters and foster carers so that the child can remain with their carers if they cannot return to their birth family. This is similar to the concurrency model, used to a much lesser extent in England. However, there is also a smaller number of children who are adopted by foster carers who are not dually approved. In 2013/14, 89 children were adopted: 48 (53%) by adopters who had been dually approved; 14 (16%) by their short-term foster carers; and four (5%) by their kinship foster carers (ARIS, 2014). Within the total group of 89 children, the average age of children adopted by their foster carers was five years and three months, compared to four years and three months for other adopted children, and there was a higher number of boys adopted. Statistics published for 2014/15 show that 53 per cent of the 72 children adopted that year were adopted by their foster carers, but in the national statistics it is not possible to know what proportion of these had been dually approved or were short-term carers.

MESSAGES FROM RESEARCH

Research into foster carers adopting children in their care has been part of wider research projects since the 1970s and 1980s, when there was an increased focus on "children who wait" and on placing "harder to place" children for adoption. It was also a feature of research that examined the impact of the introduction of adoption allowances in 1982 (Hill *et al*), which was a policy initiative partly introduced to help overcome the financial obstacles to foster carers wishing to adopt.

Research has also explored the extent to which foster carers would be willing to adopt. These findings have varied between studies: in 1976, Shaw and Lebens estimated that between one-third and one-half of long-term foster carers would be interested in adoption, whilst Rowe *et al* (1984) found that only about 20 per cent of foster carers would consider adopting, due to concerns about loss of financial support, managing children's behaviour, and a preference for the fostering role.

Another research study by Kirton *et al* (2006) looked at the motivations for and deterrents to foster carers adopting. This came out of a larger study (Kirton *et al*, 2003) on the relationship between remuneration and performance in foster care and so had a particular focus on the role of finance. For the main study, Kirton and colleagues surveyed foster carers from 21 agencies, 16 local authorities (LAs) and five independent fostering providers (IFPs) and received responses from 1,181 carers. The sample, by its nature, did not include any carers who had then ceased fostering as a result of adopting a child.

More recently, research commissioned by the DfE through the Adoption Research Initiative (Biehal *et al*, 2010) compared placement stability in different types of permanent placements including adoption by strangers, foster carers or permanent foster carers. This study looked at historical and current data and surveyed and interviewed adopters, carers and social workers from seven different local authorities.

In 2015, research on adoption disruptions (Selwyn *et al*) provided some limited data on foster carer adoptions from a dataset of all the children who had had an adoption order made in 2000/2011 and who had then experienced a disruption (see later in this chapter for more information).

The findings from these studies are described below.

Who are the foster carers who adopt and how are they supported?

Motivation and willingness of foster carers to adopt

Kirton *et al's* (2006) research showed that 436 carers (37%) had considered adopting a child whom they were fostering. However, in the 16 local authorities involved, this ranged from 24 per cent to 60 per cent of the carers who responded, and in the five IFPs this ranged from 18 per cent to 50 per cent of the carers who responded. There were local authorities where the "conversion rate" from those expressing an interest in adoption was more than half, and others where it was less than one-fifth. In IFPs, only 13 per cent of carers who had considered adopting went on to do so, representing four per cent of the IFP carers in the survey.

Kirton and colleagues estimated that about three in every eight carers had considered adopting at least one foster child and about one in eight had proceeded to adopt. The majority had adopted only one child. Carers who had fostered for longer, who regarded themselves as having certain "specialisms", and who offered a higher number and wider range of placements were found to be more likely to consider adoption. This may have been related to their opportunity to become attached to a particular child.

Kirton et al found that, equally, there was a group of carers for whom there was an essential difference between foster care and adoption that mattered to them, illustrated by the following quotes from the research: 'We did not go into fostering with a view to adopting'; 'It defeats the purpose of fostering'; 'We provide a service'; 'We are foster carers'. (p 14, 2006)

Kirton and colleagues suggested that, despite periodic attempts by the social work system to establish a clear demarcation between fostering and adoption services, fostering continues to provide a significant route into adoption and adoption has a strong resonance among foster carers, irrespective of their terms of approval. Therefore, foster carers may be an underutilised resource in terms of adoption.

Biehal et al (2010) found that carer adoption gave older children, who have often come into care at a later age, a chance of being adopted and this was also demonstrated in some of the examples given by local authorities we contacted.

In Biehal et al's research, foster carers were motivated by their own feelings of love for the child, wanting to provide them with security and stability but also a desire to protect them from the "vagaries of the care system".

> He was very attached and so was I. A couple had turned him down and I thought of this as a sign that we should be together. I'm so glad I did. (p104)

This again was a theme apparent with some of the carers and local authorities we spoke to, where carers put themselves forward to adopt when adopters had not been found, an adoption placement had disrupted or if they felt that there had been too much delay for the child.

Biehal et al found that some managers felt that the motivation for people to foster or adopt was quite different. However, in more recent research commissioned by the DfE that explored barriers and motivations to adopt or foster, there was seen to be significant overlap in the motivators for foster carers and prospective adopters, focusing on benefits for themselves but also benefits for children and society as a whole (Scott and Duncan, 2013).

In some cases, Biehal and colleagues found that the carer's decision to adopt had been prompted by the child:

There comes a point when the kids reach 10, 11, 12 and they say, 'Why haven't you adopted me?' And the foster carer will then adopt because up to that point it hasn't made any difference to them because they are totally committed to the child.
(p53)

Children adopted by their foster carers were found to have formed a strong bond prior to the adoption and to have a strong sense of belonging to their adoptive families. Although curious about their birth parents at the time of the study, the children had no reported sense of divided loyalties, and some had maintained direct contact as carers had been more open to continuing contact that had been in place while they were fostered.

Children also expressed relief at achieving the legal security of adoption where this had happened at an older age.

Oh my God, you feel like a weight's been taken off your foot...you feel absolutely brilliant in a way, you feel like you got a family that actually likes you for who you are. Like they love you for who you are, not because of what you are, it feels brilliant. (Niamh placed at 5, now 16.)
(p208)

Niamh's very much...this is my home, this is my mum and dad. I'm here until I decide otherwise and that's the way it is and that's the way it's staying. (Her carers who continue to foster)
(p209)

The strong relationships between the child and their carers prior to the adoption application contributed to the success of carer adoptions.

It was my heart, you know, because we loved her, we'd grown to love her and care for her and she felt the same...she's great and even if she wasn't great, we'd still love her because she's part of our family, you know.
(p103)

As we discuss further in Chapter 3, the strength of these relationships are a significant motivator for carers and need to be taken into consideration when plans for permanence are being made for a child.

Financial support/adoption allowances

Hill *et al* (1982) found that in the first few years after the adoption allowance schemes were introduced, the majority of allowances agreed had enabled foster carers to adopt long-term fostered children who were already in "quasi-adoption" placements. This study identified short-term carers as 'an important source of adopters' (p57).

Kirton *et al* (2006) also found that the role of financial support was significant, as 98 (62%) of the foster carers in their study who had adopted had been given an adoption allowance (including three who had adopted more than one child and so had experience of adopting both with and without an allowance). All but one of the 11 single adopters had received adoption allowances. The majority (59%) of those fostering for more than 20 years had adopted without an allowance (these may have been historic cases), but for those who had fostered for between six and 20 years, only 25 per cent had adopted without an allowance.

This research found that those carers showing interest in adoption had been assessed in the wider survey as being relatively less concerned with the financial aspects of foster care. (There was also evidence of this from within our own sample of foster carers.)

> *As far as we were concerned this child had become our daughter and we had no expectation of any financial support whatsoever.*
> FCA 3

> *My only income is through fostering. There's a sense in which I didn't really care what difficulties I might experience financially etc. as my son's welfare and chance of a good outcome were absolutely paramount. I believed, and still do, that I would weather whatever storms came as a result of my decision to adopt, for the sake of my son.*
> FCA 1

However, the continued importance of adoption allowances was highlighted by Kirton *et al*'s finding that carers with lower incomes were more likely to consider adoption.

Biehal *et al* (2010) also found that financial support was being used to facilitate the adoptions and 62 per cent of carer adopters in her study were receiving an adoption allowance.

What are the barriers to foster carers adopting?

Response from social workers and local authorities

Hill *et al* (1982) noted resistance by social workers to short-term foster carers adopting children in their care, with carers being viewed as achieving adoption "by the back door" or concern being expressed about agencies losing valuable short-term placements.

Kirton et al (2006) found that some foster carers in their 40s and 50s cited their age as a reason not to pursue adoption, either because they 'felt they were too old' or 'would be considered too old' (p144). At the time of that study this was also a common perception amongst prospective adopters, but there have been recent shifts in adoption policy which mean that agencies cannot refuse to accept a registration of interest on the grounds of a prospective adopter's age, but rather that they should assess the potential carer adopter's ability to care for the child throughout their childhood and into adulthood. This can include looking at the support available within their family networks.

In **Biehal et al's study** (2010), when social workers were asked why looked after children in the study had not been adopted, in half of the cases this was because the child was seen to be "too settled" in foster care, and local policies, resources and practice cultures were found to have had an impact on how decisions about pursuing adoption were taken, particularly for older children. The researchers queried why adoption could not have been pursued for some of these children, with appropriate financial help and post-adoption support.

Biehal and colleagues identified significant differences between agencies in the level and use of carer adoption and highlighted the impact of this on key people in that agency. They note that one local authority had seen a 'huge increase in carer adoptions' (p54) and that the manager there attributed this to a change in the authority's approach and an accompanying change in workers' responses to carers wishing to adopt.

This was also evident in discussions we had with local authorities, in which it was recognised that a change of attitude amongst managers had led to improved practice, a more positive response to carers and therefore an increase in the number of children being adopted by their carers.

Biehal *et al*'s study highlights the need to understand and challenge the variation of use of carer adoption by local authorities and for them to examine whether their policies support the appropriate use of carer adoption when it is right for the child.

Financial and adoption support

Kirton et al (2006) found that the two main reasons given separately or in combination by more than half of all the carers who had considered but not then pursued adoption were of losing financial help and support with the placement. For some carers, it was a lack of "space" in its various forms that constrained their pursuit of adoption, including where it would then lead to a reduced involvement in fostering. When long-term foster carers in this study were asked why they were reluctant to adopt children in their care, they also expressed concern at losing both financial and placement support.

WHAT RESEARCH TELLS US ABOUT STABILITY OF CARER ADOPTION PLACEMENTS

The most recent research on adoption disruptions (Selwyn *et al*, 2015) provides some limited data on carer adoptions from a dataset of all the children who had an adoption order made in 2000–2011 and who then experienced a disruption. Selwyn and colleagues found that foster carers were more likely to apply for special guardianship orders and residence orders (now child arrangements orders) rather than adoption orders, but that minority ethnic children who were adopted were more likely to be adopted by foster carers than by "stranger" adopters.

The children adopted by their foster carers entered care aged under two (a similar age profile to those adopted by strangers) and were on average 2.4 years old when they were first placed with foster carers. However, children adopted by their carers waited significantly longer – an average of two years before their foster placement became an adoptive placement, with one-quarter waiting more than three years. By the time of the adoption order, the average age of children adopted by their foster carers was 5.3, compared with an age of 3.8 for children adopted by stranger adopters.

Selwyn *et al* noted that the delays may have been because:

- foster carers stepped in to adopt when adopters could not be found;
- 'negotiations for acceptable support packages were lengthy' (p36); or
- the local authority was not, at least initially, supportive of the foster carer's application to adopt.

Similar findings on the delays were evident in Selwyn's equivalent study of adoption disruption in Wales (Selwyn and Meakings, 2015).

This finding supports the need for early consideration of carer adoption during care planning and for support issues to be addressed at an earlier stage.

Selwyn *et al* also noted that 'it has been assumed that foster carer adoptions are more stable than adoptions by strangers' (2015, p35). This view is based on the fact that carers would have a well-established relationship with the child and would therefore have based their decision to adopt on a realistic view of the child's difficulties. However, Selwyn *et al's* initial finding was that carer adoptions were not more stable than "stranger" adoptions and that children who were fostered prior to adoption were more likely to have an adoption disruption. This was thought to be influenced by the facts that:

- adoption managers were more likely to report foster carer than stranger adoptive disruptions, as those who had continued to foster would still be in touch with the local authority;

- the withdrawal of support post-order from foster carers could increase the risk of disruption;

- foster carers may adopt children with more special needs than children adopted by stranger adopters; and

- those children had waited longer for the foster placements to become their adoptive placement (than children adopted by "stranger" adopters).

However, once other variables were taken into account, Selwyn *et al* found that there was no evidence that carer adoptions were more (or less) stable than adoptions by "stranger" adopters.

KEY POINTS

- There has been no significant change in the percentage of children being adopted by their foster carers in the last 15 years, despite political interest and government reform.

- The average age of children adopted by their foster carers is higher than that of children adopted by strangers, and there is some anecdotal evidence that this provides a route for permanence for children usually seen as "harder to place".

- There is potential learning from the positive shifts in attitudes towards carer adoptions from evidence and research in the USA.

- There is potential for more foster carers to consider adoption if perceived barriers are removed.

- The attitudes of key people in the local authority can have a positive (or negative) impact on foster carers coming forward to adopt.

- Financial support can be a key factor in enabling foster carers to adopt and agencies should consider how they use their discretion in determining these allowances.

- Adoption support needs to be considered and agreed as part of the package to give foster carers confidence in offering adoption for older children and to reduce the risks of disruption.

Chapter 2
The legislative framework

ENGLAND

Routes to adoption of a child by their foster carer

There are two routes for foster carers wishing to adopt a child in their care.

- They can apply to adopt and be assessed as adopters under the Adoption Agency Regulations 2005, as amended by the Adoption Agencies (Miscellaneous Amendments) Regulations 2013.* Statutory Adoption Guidance 2013 provides further information about how the regulations should be applied.

- Alternatively, they can make a direct application to court to adopt the child; this is known as a non-agency adoption and is covered by the Adoption and Children Act 2002[†] (ACA) and Volume 1 of the Statutory Guidance on court orders (DfE, 2014c), set out below.

The main focus of this guide is on progressing agency adoption placements, but the following information sets out the legislative framework and issues for non-agency adoptions.

Non-agency adoptions

The route for foster carers making a direct adoption application to court is the same as that used by relatives, step-parents, private foster carers or special guardians. Whilst it can be seen as a more timely way of achieving an adoption order, there can be disadvantages for the foster carer and the child/ren adopted by them, particularly in their eligibility for adoption support services if the child has not had a plan for adoption agreed and so is not deemed to be an "agency adoptive child".

In April 2014, Statutory Guidance on court orders and pre-proceedings (Vol 1 SG) (DfE) was issued, setting out the process. In the highlighted

---

* See www.legislation.gov.uk/uksi/2013/985/made.

† See www.legislation.gov.uk/ukpga/2002/38/contents.

text below there is encouragement to use the adoption agency route if the application is supported by the agency.

> If (when the local authority receives a notice of intention to adopt) the foster carer had not previously discussed with the local authority their wish to adopt before notice is given, the local authority should give it serious consideration and ensure that the foster carer is offered information and counselling. **If adoption is already the plan for the child, and the local authority considers that the foster carer may be suitable to be approved as an adoptive parent, the foster carer can be assessed using the fast-track procedure under Regulation 30F of the Adoption Agencies Regulations 2005. Any application for an adoption order by the foster carer made after they have been assessed and considered suitable to adopt, would proceed as an agency adoption.**
> DfE, 2014c, Chap 5.21

A foster carer can make a direct application to the court once the child they want to adopt has been living with them for one year. If the child has been with them for less than a year, they would have to apply to the court for leave to make an application. Where a foster carer decides to make a direct application to court, and where necessary obtains the leave of the court, they must give formal notice of their intention to apply for an adoption order to the local authority *where they live*. The notice must be given between three months and two years before the application is made to the court. If the local authority is not the local authority which placed the child, it must then inform that local authority in writing within seven days. This will enable the local authority responsible for the child to decide whether it will support or oppose the application.

Once notification has been received, the local authority is not allowed to remove the child from the foster carer without the leave of the court. If the local authority has concerns about the care of the child, they can make an application to remove the child under Part 18 of the Family Procedure Rules 2010.

The process then followed depends on whether there is a placement order made on the child:

> If the local authority is not authorised to place the child for adoption, the local authority must immediately consider the plan for the child and ascertain the wishes and feelings of the child and birth parents. If the local authority considers that adoption may be appropriate, it must follow the procedure set out in Part 3 of the Adoption Agencies Regulations 2005.
>
> If the local authority issues a placement order application before the foster carer's adoption application has been heard, it is open to the court to adjourn the placement order application and proceed to hear the foster carer's adoption application. In this case the foster carer's application would still technically be a non-agency one but for the

purposes of adoption support, the child in these circumstances falls within the definition of an 'agency adoptive child' unless the local authority opposes the application.

Alternatively, the court may adjourn the foster carer's adoption application and hear the placement order application first so that, if the placement order is granted, the foster carer's adoption application can proceed as an agency application.

DfE, 2014c, Chap 5.23-24

Adoption support for non-agency adoptions

There are important considerations for foster carers looking to adopt through a non-agency route. These are set out in Adoption Statutory Guidance.

The foster carer needs to understand the eligibility for adoption support. If the agency has not placed the child for adoption with them and the foster carer applies directly to court for an adoption order that the local authority opposes, they and the child will be limited in their eligibility under the Adoption Support Services Regulations 2005 to counselling, advice and information only. However, if the local authority supports the application to the court for an adoption order, the foster carer and the child will be eligible for assessment of their adoption support needs as is the case for any looked after child.

DfE, 2013, 2.39

Where a foster carer applies to adopt a child that they have been looking after and the local authority opposes the application, the local authority is not required to meet the legal costs of the foster carer. This is because the authority has not placed the child for adoption with the foster carer, and so the child does not fall within the definition of an 'agency adoptive child'.

DfE, 2013, 6.65

Foster carers may be able to obtain help with their legal costs from the Legal Aid Agency, provided that they satisfy the means and merits tests.

Children adopted through a non-agency adoption route and their adoptive family are only entitled to counselling, advice and information under the Adoption Support Services Regulations 2005. However, local authorities do have discretion to also offer 'services to prevent disruption...and financial support could be provided if the local authority considered this appropriate' (DfE, 2013, 6.5). Foster carers adopting through this route should be made aware of this and encouraged to contact their local authority if they need adoption support in the future.

Local authorities that wish to support a foster carer in applying for a non-agency adoption can therefore provide adoption support services that are deemed to be in the best interests of the child. They can also provide adoption support services to carer adopters to prevent disruption. Decisions about what support can be provided should also be informed by the needs of the child. The implications for all parties need to be carefully considered by agencies and carers when an application for a non-agency adoption is being proposed.

Agency adoptions

The assessment and approval of foster carers as adopters is covered by the Adoption Agencies Regulations 2005, as amended in 2013 (DfE).

When a foster carer decides to apply to adopt a child in their care, Statutory Guidance sets out that:

> Foster carers who express an interest in adopting children in their care should be advised that the adoption procedures apply in their case as in any other.
> DfE, 2013, 2.38.

It also sets out that:

> Their assessment will be in respect of their suitability to adopt generally and that, if they are approved, their suitability to adopt a specific child or children will be addressed separately as part of the matching process.
> DfE, 2013, 2.40

Once a Registration of Interest (ROI) has been accepted by the adoption agency, agencies should follow their usual processes for assessment, taking account of the specific expectations regarding the assessment of foster carers as adopters, as set out below:

> There is a fast-track process for certain adopters and foster carers who can bypass Stage One and enter the process at Stage Two. They should receive a tailored assessment (which may include elements of Stage One where the agency considers it necessary) to take account of such factors as their previous experience of fostering in general and experience of the differing needs of the children they have previously fostered.
> DfE, 2013, 2.36

Information sharing

Regulation 32(6) of the 2011 Fostering Services Regulations requires fostering services to share information to support the assessment of a person's suitability to foster or adopt, if requested to do so by the fostering service or adoption agency undertaking the assessment. The information to be shared is set out as:

> The report of the original assessment of the person's suitability to foster or adopt (if it is considered by the body requesting the information to be recent enough to be relevant); a copy of the report of the last review of the individual's continuing suitability to foster or adopt and any other review report considered useful to understanding the person's current

suitability to foster or adopt; details of any concerns about standards of practice and what if anything is being done/has been done to address them; details of allegations made against the foster carer/adopter or their household members (taking into account guidance at paragraph 3.79 of the Children Act 1989 Guidance, Volume 4: Fostering Services); and any other information considered to be relevant to the assessment of the person's suitability to foster/adopt.

Requests from the adoption agency for access to information should be accompanied by the written consent of the applicant to the sharing of their information. The receiving fostering service should acknowledge the request within two working days; seek consent from all others referred to in the information within five working days; and the information, redacted where necessary, should be provided within 15 working days.

Adoption Statutory Guidance also provides for the approval and match to be heard at the same panel, prior to the agency decision-maker deciding on the approval of the carers:

In appropriate cases, and to avoid unnecessary delay, the recommendation as to the child's placement can be made at the same panel meeting at which a recommendation has been made in respect of the child and/or the prospective adopter.

However, each recommendation must be considered separately. This means that the panel must consider whether the prospective adopter is suitable to adopt any child and if so, go on to consider whether to recommend that the particular child should be placed for adoption with that prospective adopter. Making recommendations in this way may be appropriate where a child is living with foster carers who wish to adopt them.
DfE, 2013, 8.26

Support for agency adoptions

Children adopted by their foster carers as an agency adoption placement and their adoptive parents will be entitled to all the adoption support provision set out in legislation. In addition, Adoption Support Regulations (ASR) 2005 and Statutory Guidance make specific provision in relation to financial support for foster carers adopting children whom they have cared for.

This means that, although usually local authorities cannot include any remuneration or fees in their financial support to adopters, an exception is made for former foster carers to give them time to adjust to their new circumstances:

ASR 9 provides, however, that where the adopter previously fostered the child they are adopting, and they received remuneration in the financial

support paid to them as the child's foster parent, the local authority may continue to pay remuneration for a transitional period of two years from the date of the adoption order. This can continue for longer than two years if the local authority considers the case to be exceptional. The purpose of the transitional provision is to enable local authorities to maintain payments to foster parents who go on to adopt, at the same rate as they received when they were fostering the child. This is intended to give the family time to adjust to their new circumstances.
DfE, 2013, 6.63/6.64

As will be discussed further in Chapter 4, it is important that local authorities have clear policies about the financial support they will provide to carer adopters, and discussions about financial support should be held at an early stage, with authorities exercising discretion according to the needs of the child.

WALES

Adoption by foster carers is covered in the Adoption Agencies (Wales) Regulations 2005 and accompanying Statutory Guidance. There was also some additional guidance set out in Practice Guidance published in July 2007 on Preparing and Assessing Prospective Adopters.

When foster carers adopt they will need to consider carefully whether they should continue to foster; they will need to consider any birth children, the adopted child and any potential foster children.
Welsh Assembly Government (WAG), 2007, 50

Foster carers may wish to be considered as prospective adopters for child(ren) placed with them. They should formally notify the local authority of their wish to be considered as prospective adopters, the notification acknowledged and the process of adoption assessment fully explained to them.

In any event local authority foster carers who wish to adopt the child they are fostering and who has lived with them for one year must notify their local authority of their intention to apply to adopt that child, so that a report can be prepared. They may then apply direct to the court without needing the agreement of the local authority which is responsible for the looked after child. When notified, the local authority has a duty to investigate the circumstances of the application and to prepare a report for the court.
WAG, 2007, 51

Where the local authority has previously assessed and approved foster carers, it will know much about them. However, they were assessed for a different caring role and their adoption assessment should consider anew their parenting capacities and skills for meeting the child's needs throughout their childhood and beyond. It may be necessary to arrange for a new medical report: the agency should seek the advice of its medical adviser.

If two years have elapsed since the foster carers' last enhanced CRB (now DBS) checks, these will need to be renewed. New references will be needed as they are now being assessed as proposed adopters for a particular child.
WAG, 2007, 52

Adoption support should help to ensure that placements are not prevented solely for financial reasons. Foster carers adopting a child already living with them may get financial help during the transition to adoption.
WAG, 2007, 53

The Practice Guidance sets out that foster carers who make a formal application to adopt children in their care should receive information and preparation appropriate to their particular circumstances. It also notes that National Minimum Standards (Standard 4.5) state that foster carers wishing to adopt a child they are caring for are entitled to the same preparation as other adopters and will be assessed within four months.

NORTHERN IRELAND

Major reform of adoption legislation in Northern Ireland is anticipated, and, at the time of writing, the consultation process for the draft Adoption and Children Bill was imminent. It is anticipated that the new legislation will largely mirror the Adoption and Children Act (England and Wales) 2002 and its accompanying guidance and regulations.

The options for legal permanence for children who remain with their foster carers or with kinship carers are more limited as the option of special guardianship is not available. This may be a factor in the number of children currently being adopted by their kinship carers and the higher percentage adopted by foster carers.

The Adoption Regional Policy and Procedures require Trusts to discuss plans to place a child for adoption with their foster carer and to give priority to responding to adoption applications from existing foster/ kinship carers in respect of a specific child, to avoid delay in care planning for the child.

Currently, adoption support is delivered under the Adoption (Northern Ireland) Order 1987, which does not specifically address the support needs of older children placed for adoption or those of foster families who adopt a child in their care.

Financial support may be available under the Adoption Allowances Regulations (Northern Ireland) 1996 under Regulation 2(2)(a):

Where the adoption agency is satisfied that the child has established a strong and important relationship with the adopters before the adoption order is made.

Eligibility for adoption allowances are means-dependent and subject to annual review of both the child's circumstances and their adoptive parent's financial situation.

SCOTLAND

The Adoption and Children (Scotland) Act 2007 provides the legislative framework for adoption by foster carers in Scotland. It provides for two types of adoption: namely, an agency adoption and a non-agency adoption. The distinction is important in terms of the age of the child, the length of time the child has to have resided with the carer, and the type of report prepared by the local authority to be lodged in court.

Foster carers planning to adopt a child may have had that child placed with them with a view to their adopting them, in which case an agency adoption would ensue. For this to happen, certain criteria must have been satisfied, namely:

- the plan for the child is adoption and this has been recommended by the agency's adoption panel and formally decided on by the agency; and

- the proposed adopters have been approved as adopters by an adoption agency; and

- the adoption panel has recommended the match of the specific child and the specific approved adopters and this has been formally agreed by an adoption agency, usually the child's agency, so that the child is treated as "placed" for adoption.

If the child was placed with the carers in a fostering arrangement and the carers subsequently wish to adopt the child, this would be treated as a non-agency adoption. This is because the child was not placed with them with a view to adoption and the above criteria were not met.

Court process

The court processes for both types of adoptions are the same, but the report written by the placing agency is done so under different sections of the 2007 Act, namely s.17 for an agency adoption and s.19 for a non-agency adoption.

may continue if considered necessary because of 'the exceptional needs of the child or any other exceptional circumstances'.

ISSUES RAISED IN RELEVANT CASE LAW

The following cases involve children who have been adopted by their foster carers in England. We have selected these because they highlight the importance of having clear processes for identifying and approving situations where being adopted by their foster carer is the best outcome for the child. They show how courts take account of the particular significance of the relationships formed between the carer adopter and the child. They also demonstrate some of the complexities that need to be considered in relation to the views of birth family members, differing views of professionals, the importance of identifying any interest from foster carers prior to progressing with other options, and determining contact plans that take account of the child's needs, existing relationships and the views of the prospective adopters.

Re A (A Minor) [2007] EWCA Civ 1383 (21 December 2007)

Appeal by foster mother against a refusal to allow her leave to apply to adopt a child currently in her care. Appeal allowed.

This case featured a foster mother who had a girl, A, placed with her at six days old in March 2007 and who was nine months old at the time of application. A placement order was made in October 2007. A had only had her home with the foster mother for eight months, so the foster mother required leave to apply for an adoption order as the local authority decided not to progress her application to adopt. She had previously adopted a child in her care and there were some concerns about her capacity to offer long-term care for this child alongside her other children.

Her application was being supported by the child's birth mother, although she had not consented to the making of a placement order, and by the Children's Guardian who initially felt that in the light of A's bond with the foster mother and her other children, it would be better for A to remain with the foster mother than for her to be moved to another adoptive family. He later modified his view to say that her suitability should be tested through her application to the court to adopt.

The judgement sets out the various reasons given by the local authority for deciding not to accept the foster carer's application to adopt and the carer's responses to these issues. These raised some questions about how the initial assessment that was completed led to the local authority deciding not to pursue her application. The judge criticised the length of time taken by the local authority to respond to a letter written by the foster carer when she was told they would not consider her application, and the judgement noted that whilst social workers properly advised the foster mother that she could seek legal advice, she was incorrectly told that as A had not been in her care for a year, she could not apply to the court for an adoption order and was not made aware that she could seek leave to do so.

Within the reporting, there is information about the differing views held by the local authority and the carer about her motivation. The local authority had felt that:

> *Motivation to foster and adopt is different. She came forward to foster* [A]. *If she wants to adopt, she can contact the adoption team to be assessed as an adopter –* [the foster mother] *indicating that she does not want to adopt in general but wants to adopt* [A] *specifically as her children are attached to her and wanting her to remain with family.*

The foster carer's response to this highlights the differences in motivation for a foster carer seeking to adopt but challenges why this is not seen as valid:

> *In reference to* [the social worker's] *suggestion that I get assessed and "on the list instead of jumping the queue", again I will say as a previous adopter and a foster carer with 11 years' experience, I feel that if I can offer this child a loving home and stable environment which she is already accustomed to, this will of course prevent any disruption in her routine/life. The child's needs are paramount and I have already proved to be an excellent carer of this and other children who have been placed with me and my family. I have also successfully adopted before, a child with special needs who has achieved more than it was ever thought possible due to her upbringing before she was placed with me. As a family, we feel that* [A] *fits perfectly into our lives, she is a very happy, contented little girl who is attached to both us and my extended family and friends. We love her very much and have no doubt that she will continue to thrive with the love, care and attention that she receives on a daily basis.*

The issues raised in this case highlighted the importance of addressing whether a carer is wishing to be considered at an early stage of care planning. There is also some evidence, as highlighted in research, of social workers having looked at this carer's application and motivation and comparing it to a stranger carer rather than accepting that the motivation and circumstances leading to her application will be different and equally valid.

Coventry City Council v PGO & Others [2011] EWCA Civ 729 (22 June 2011)

Judgement in appeal determining (a) whether the County Court has power to injunct a local authority from removing a child from the care of foster carers who wish to adopt him, when the local authority has a placement order and wishes to place the child with prospective adopters; and (b) when a child becomes "placed" for adoption.

This case concerned two children: L, aged two, and C, aged one, who were placed with short-term foster carers. Placement orders had been made in June 2010 and there had been some delay before the local authority had identified prospective adopters, who were matched and were in the process of introductions with the children prior to a planned move of the children on 23 February 2011.

However, it subsequently emerged that the foster carers had been taking legal advice, and on the eve of the planned move they applied without notice for adoption orders and revocation of the placement orders. There was a dispute between the parties as to whether the foster carers had ever previously indicated that they would not seek to adopt the children; however, it was accepted that the foster carers had not given the local authority the requisite three months' notice of their intention to apply for adoption orders. An emergency hearing took place the day after the applications, at which the local authority agreed not to remove the children, pending a hearing. At the instigation of the prospective adopters, contact between them and the children also ceased and they later withdrew.

Evidence showed that at a very early stage the children's social worker had expressed doubts to the foster carers about their chance of successfully applying to adopt the children, although they had later been given a number of other opportunities to consider their position.

This case highlights the importance of local authorities having a clear policy about foster carers adopting, which addresses how carers are given the opportunity to express their interest at an early stage and the importance of a fully considered response to any expressions of interest.

Re S and T (Children) [2014] EWCC B21 (Fam) (26 February 2014)

Consideration of applications for care orders and placement orders

In this case, the local authority was applying for a care order and placement order for two children who were in placement with their foster carer, H. During the course of the care proceedings, it became clear that the current foster carer would be in a position to adopt the children and this was being supported by the local authority, which had reached a financial agreement that had enabled the foster carer to put themself forward as an adopter.

The judge agreed that the grounds were met for making a care order, but because the birth parents had said that they would support the foster carer's application to adopt the children, the judge felt that their support of the plan would be 'a hugely important factor for children, parents, and H, and likely to contribute to the stability of the placement in the long term and that should be recognised'. The judge felt that it was not appropriate to dispense with parental consent to adoption in such circumstances where the parents may not wish to consent to a placement order, but would consent to an adoption application made by H. He proposed instead to invite the birth parents to consider granting advance consent under s.20 to adoption of the children by H. He agreed to adjourn the local authority's application rather than dismiss it, so that if consent was not forthcoming he could reconsider the application and the issue of whether to dispense with parental consent.

This case raises an interesting question about the consideration and involvement of birth parents when a carer adoption is being proposed. There are some situations where birth parents are not made aware that the foster carer is the proposed adopter due to concerns about security and safety. However, where birth parents are aware of the proposed carer adoption and are in full support, this case would suggest that birth parents should be given the opportunity to give specific consent to adoption before the placement order is applied for.

Re N (A Child) (Adoption Order) [2014] EWFC 1491 (2 May 2014)

Consideration of special guardianship orders against adoption orders, particularly in light of Re B-S [2013] EWCA Civ 813

This case concerned a five-year-old child with significant disabilities who had been in the care of her foster carers since birth. Her father accepted that he could not care for the child, but opposed the foster carers' adoption application, suggesting instead that a special guardianship order could be made. The prospective carer adopters had argued that they:

> ...want her to become a full member of their family for the rest of her life. They see this as particularly important in view of her disabilities and the likelihood that she will be dependent on them long after she has attained her majority.

The court dispensed with the father's consent and, using the *Re B-S* balancing exercise, it was argued that the child required adoption to legally secure the relationship for the rest of her life, rather than an order that remained in force until she reached 18. The court also refused to make a contact order as the carer adopters were committed to facilitating face-to-face contact up to four times a year and it was felt that making the arrangement fixed would risk unsettling the child with possible future applications being made to vary the order.

This case gives clarity to the importance of the local authority and the foster carers being clear about their reasoning for deciding that adoption is the right route to permanence, taking account of a child's specific needs. Whilst this is mainly an issue for care planning, inevitably where the local authority wants to support a child remaining permanently with their foster carer, it is important that their reasoning is clearly set out as required by Re B-S and that the carer's views are also considered and included.

Re SSM (A Child) [2015] EWHC 327 (Fam)

Application by father for leave to oppose an adoption order, made pursuant to s.47(5) of the Adoption and Children Act 2002. Application refused and adoption order made.

This involved a six-year-old child being adopted by his foster carers with whom he had lived since birth. His father applied for leave to oppose the adoption based on his change of circumstances – namely that he had a new relationship without domestic abuse (he had been violent towards his previous partner) and two children with whom he did not live but did care for without difficulty. Whilst the court accepted that this was a change in circumstances, the judge then went on to explore whether the father would have any chance of success in opposing the adoption. There was a challenge from the father that the foster carers had initially been persuaded into adoption:

> We requested that SSM be placed with us as a long-term foster child but were told that due to his hyperactivity he would be moved to younger foster carers, but we could adopt SSM as we were not too old for adoption, subject to being approved. We found this logic extremely strange and nonsensical, but could not allow the potential risk to SSM of being moved from our care. We felt the local authority emotionally gave us no choice but to secure SSM's placement by way of an adoption order.

However, it was reported that: 'Notwithstanding their initial stance, the prospective adopters strongly wish an adoption order to be made'. The judge found that there was no chance of the child being returned to his father's care and that the child needed security of adoption in the family where he was settled and had clearly stated that he wanted to remain there. The prospective adopters were also open to ongoing contact between the child and his father and other siblings who were remaining in care. Leave to oppose was not granted and the adoption order was later made.

Although this case raises some questions about how the plan for adoption by the foster carers was reached, it also highlights that, with an older child, the child's views should be considered when thinking about the possibility and future success of a carer adoption. It also highlights the importance of an openness to contact with birth family members that may not have been present in another non-related placement.

KEY POINTS

- Clear policies for processing foster carer adoptions will ensure that all staff have a shared understanding of the process and give a consistent message to carers considering adoption.

- Foster carers' motivation will differ from that of "stranger" adopters – this should be understood and not be viewed negatively by social workers.

- Where a birth parent supports adoption by a foster carer, the option of specific consent to adoption could be explored.

- Foster carers can be more open to supporting contact with birth family members and siblings based on their existing relationships.

Chapter 3
Preparation, assessment and approval of carer adopters

THE CARE PLANNING PROCESS

In cases where a local authority has decided that adoption will be their primary plan to achieve permanence for a child, Adoption Statutory Guidance is clear about the importance of avoiding delay and early care planning.

Unnecessary delays in the adoption process may have an adverse effect on the child's development and welfare and may reduce their chances of being adopted. The child's need for a permanent home must be addressed and a permanence plan should be made as early as possible; well before and no later than the second statutory review (four months after the child becomes looked after)...The adoption scorecards expect that children for whom adoption is the plan will be placed with their prospective adoptive family, on average, within 14 months of entering care by 2016.
DfE, 2013, 1.1

Family finding should begin as soon as adoption is under consideration, and before the ADM decides that the child should be placed for adoption or a placement order is made.
DfE, 2013, 3.17

Therefore, we suggest that it is important for social workers to consider at an early stage in their care planning whether the child's foster carer would: a) want to be considered; and b) be able to offer an appropriate placement. This would then give the carers time to consider the range of issues involved, in addition to their attachment and commitment to the child, and give the local authority enough time to consider the viability of an application from the carers. It would also help to avoid last-minute applications by foster carers, which can disrupt potential adoption placements and cause distress to all involved, as shown in the case discussed in the previous chapter, *Coventry City Council v PGO & Others* [2011].

These issues should be discussed at LAC Reviews and in other forums such as permanency planning meetings in an open and transparent way. It should be noted that many foster carers will not want to adopt, and these discussions should therefore be presented in a way that enables them to come forward where they have a strong motivation to do so, but does not in any way pressure them into making an application.

There may be situations where the local authority view is that adoption is the right plan for the child, but the carers want to make a permanent commitment to the child through another route, such as special guardianship or long-term fostering. It would be important to fully explore the carer's reasons for this and whether they are fully aware of the potential support that can be offered by the local authority. These situations will need to be carefully considered and a balancing of the advantages and disadvantages for the child of the different outcomes, as set out in *Re B-S*, will be needed.

Prior to assessment

Prior to commencing any assessment of foster carers who wish to adopt, the local authority must be very clear about any internal protocols, custom, practice and policies that may impact on this process. A clear and robust departmental policy on foster carers adopting should be available, so that carer adopters all receive the same treatment should they decide to express an interest in adopting a child in their care, and so that all social workers follow the same practice. A sample checklist of issues to consider when foster carers are considering adoption is reproduced in Appendix 4. Team managers, Independent Reviewing Officers, supervising social workers in the fostering service and local authority adoption workers should all be aware of this policy within their respective agencies and should give foster carers access to the information at an early stage of interest. In the case of IFPs, it is suggested that placing local authorities make IFPs aware of their policy during the commissioning process, so that there is a clear understanding between all workers, should an IFP foster carer decide that they wish to be assessed as a prospective adopter for a child later on in the placement.

The agency must be open and transparent in its dealings with all potential carer adopters and issues such as age, health, space in the home, attitudes of extended family members, household composition, location, pets, fostering alongside adoption, etc, should be discussed prior to accepting any Registration of Interest (ROI). The discussions with the foster carer should be fully documented and any possible difficulties discussed at an early stage. The IFP and its carers must be clear that the adoption agency will not automatically accept their ROI unless there is evidence that these discussions have taken place and that the carers meet the agency's criteria for an adopter assessment.

Foster carers should be advised that prior to registering an interest in any child in their care, they should have considered these relevant issues and have had discussions with their supervising social worker and the child's social worker. Where possible, they should raise their interest within the LAC review process with the Independent Reviewing Officer so it can be considered when decisions are being made about the child's Care Plan and options for that child.

If the Care Plan is agreed to be adoption and the foster family feels committed to this child, they should write to the child's local authority expressing their desire to be assessed as prospective adopters. This should be treated as the ROI and the local authority must decide whether or not it will proceed with an adoption assessment. The local authority may want to undertake an initial visit to enable them to reach a decision about proceeding to an assessment. Where the local authority is unable to accept the carer's ROI, a letter explaining the reasons for this decision should be issued within five days. At this stage, the carers do not have recourse to a review of this decision by the Independent Review Mechanism, although they can make representations to the agency or through the local authority's complaints procedure. Where a decision is made not to accept the ROI, there needs to be recognition of the support the foster carers will need from their supervising social worker if they are continuing to care for the child while other plans are being progressed. Should the local authority or the foster carers decide at this point that they cannot continue to care for the child whilst new plans are developed, there would need to be a planned move preceded by a Child Care Review in line with s.4 of the Care Planning, Placement and Case Review (CPPR) Regulations 2015.

Some local authorities ask carers to wait until the outcome of an initial visit/planning meeting has been determined before submitting their ROI. It is important that this does not disadvantage carers or introduce any significant delay into the process.

Where the agency wishes to proceed with an assessment and accepts the ROI, then the requirements of Stage One of the adoption assessment process should commence alongside the Stage Two assessment.

The assessment process

Once the ROI is accepted, a carer adopter application should be fast-tracked so that Stages One and Two of the assessment process will be followed at the same time, taking four months to complete in total.

An assessment agreement should be completed with the carers (an example is given in Appendix 3) at the beginning of the assessment process. It is advisable for a panel date to be booked in for the recommendation for approval. Many agencies will also book the match between the child and the carer adopters at the same panel following on from the approval.

In Stage One, all the statutory checks, for example, medicals, Disclosure and Barring Service (DBS) checks and new personal references, should be completed. It is important to take new personal references to evidence the relationship between the child and the carer adopter and the nature of the attachment that has developed. In situations where carer adopters have complex health issues or there are concerns raised by either statutory checks or references, the process may take a little longer than four months. These reasons will need to be recorded and clarified within the assessment document. Applicants should be clear what the delays are.

Should the issues raised in statutory checks lead to the local authority deciding that they cannot pursue the application, then the applicants must be informed in writing in a timely manner that the assessment will not continue as a result of the Stage One information gathered. As the concerns are Stage One information, the carer adopter applicants will not have recourse to the Independent Review Mechanism. This may then pose problems for the placement in cases where there is conflict with the carers, and serious consideration will need to be given to the course of action that is then pursued. In situations where the carer does not accept the outcome, this may lead to foster carers deciding to make an application to the court in their own right (non-agency adoption, as discussed in Chapter 2).

There may be slightly different approaches to the preparation and assessment of foster carers wishing to adopt, depending on how long ago they were assessed as foster carers and what terms of approval they originally held. Should the foster carer be registered with a different fostering provider from the adoption agency, it is expected that there will be clarity about sharing information between agencies, as set out in Statutory Guidance and referred to in Chapter 2. It is therefore advisable that agencies develop a clear process for managing applications from an IFP carer as part of their policy.

In Appendix 2, flowcharts demonstrate how Leeds City Council and Essex County Council organised their carer adopter application process in 2015, and the outline of a report requested from the carer adopter's supervising social worker is also included.

Some of the responses we received indicated that carer adopters found the assessment process very difficult, which has highlighted for us the importance of workers approaching these assessments with an open mind.

We were expected to undertake all the training and preparation classes that are taken by non-foster carer adopters. No information from the fostering file was considered and the process started from scratch. It

was a difficult, intrusive, time-consuming process with a worker who, when challenged, admitted that she didn't agree with either transracial or foster carer adoptions!
FCA 3

SPECIFIC ISSUES TO BE CONSIDERED IN CARER ADOPTER APPLICATIONS

Assessing an individual or family who have an existing relationship with a child does require some additional elements within the Prospective Adopter's Report (PAR) and also within the Adoption Placement Report (APR). Appendix 2 in *Undertaking an Adoption Assessment* (Dibben, 2013) elaborates on this, and suggests that the PAR assessor should complete an interview with household members to explore the impact that adopting this child will have on existing family members. Issues such as inheritance are important for families to consider at an early stage.

Dibben also suggests that clarity about the motivation to adopt this particular child is of great significance. Is the decision to adopt solely from the foster carers, or have they been subjected to pressure from others, such as the local authority? Do they understand the differences in the role and responsibilities of adopters from those of foster carers? Do they recognise the lifelong nature of adoption?

Evidence of the carer's ability to provide good quality care for the child will need to be considered. Has the child made progress in their care? Has the carer managed challenges appropriately along the way? Has contact been an issue? What is the carer's view of the child's history and journey so far?

If the child does not share the same ethnicity, religion or culture as the foster carer, the assessment should explore what efforts have been made to address any issues that may have arisen so far.

Whilst these are evidently matters to be considered more fully in the match (APR and Adoption Support Plan), it is imperative that such questions are asked early on so that the foster family is absolutely clear about the requirements of adoptive parenting and what will be considered throughout the assessment. These topics may form part of the Assessment Agreement Plan.

Motivation

The assessor should understand why the carer adopters feel that they have made a commitment to this child, particularly if the foster family has previously looked after a number of children. Has the child been waiting for an adoptive family for some time and the foster family feels sorry for the child? Does the child have significant needs that the carer feels only they can meet? Is the child very young and the carers cannot bear the pain of them moving on? Has the child themselves expressed the wish to remain in the family and be adopted by them?

Occasionally, foster families can be put under pressure by well-meaning professionals: the Children's Guardian or IRO who feels that the child should not experience another move; the child's social worker who can see the improvements in the child's behaviour and social presentation; health professionals who see physical and emotional improvements. Pressure can also come from friends and family who perhaps do not know the child's previous history or recognise the possibility of developmental uncertainty and possible implications of contact with birth family members in the longer term.

However, often the carer adopters will describe the bond between themselves and the child and the affection between them as being a primary driver.

> *I had fostered lots of children; whilst I always found it hard when those children left my care, I hadn't really considered adopting any of them...I felt an almost immediate bond with the girls and when their care plan changed I had no reservations at all about asking to be considered as an adoptive parent for them.*
> FCA 6

> *Because the first little boy had several people look at his CPR and decide not to proceed, and we as a family all felt we could become his forever family. And the other little boy had an adoption breakdown and we all have strong attachments, and because of his health issues he has a particularly strong attachment to myself, so we wanted to offer him a safe and loving environment.*
> FCA 14

Understanding the emotional journey that the carer has made to reach the decision to apply to adopt this child will help the worker to analyse whether their motivation will translate into a strong commitment to the child. Work by Quinton (2012) and more recently Simmonds (2014) highlights that commitment is fundamental to the success of a match. Simmonds identifies that:

> *Commitment will evolve over time and is one of the clearest qualities identifiable in adopters. It also has a dynamic quality to it where it is supported by a range of resources, including key relationships that support, sustain and inform.*
> (p4)

The carer adopters below described their emotional journeys in coming to the decision to adopt.

J is 50 years old and leads an active lifestyle. She is a physically active woman who enjoys the outdoors, walking the dogs and exploring a local national park as a family. A healthy diet is something she promotes within the family, frequently using produce harvested from the family allotment. She also believes that being physically active and engaging in different things is important not just for her physical fitness but also well-being and stimulation.
(Taken from a PAR written in 2015)

Whether or not a carer smokes is evidently of significance and should have been addressed when the fostering placement was made. Where possible, people should be supported with smoking cessation programmes, but if a carer is not prepared to give up, then discussions about the child's health and well-being need to continue. In *Re A*, the fact that the carer smoked was one of the reasons given for not pursuing a placement with her – her response was that although she did not smoke in front of the child, she was 'willing to receive treatment to help stop smoking if it is deemed to be a serious issue'.

There is currently much debate on the impact of the use of e-cigarettes and the influence they may have on children taking up the smoking habit. CoramBAAF has produced guidance on this that should be referred to during the assessment (see www.baaf.org.uk/node/7583).

If there are any concerns that the foster carer's health is impaired to the extent that they cannot safely care for a child or young person, then this is a matter for the fostering provider to address openly and transparently, but it may be that the issues only arise when the potential for a more permanent placement is considered. Where it is clear that the fostering provider has not formally addressed such issues with the carer, then this would need to be part of any initial discussion about adoption.

When foster carers wishing to adopt the child in their care have been turned down on the grounds of their health and lifestyle, they are likely to then ask the question, 'If I am fit enough to foster this child and have been doing so for so long, why am I suddenly not healthy enough to adopt?' This is a situation that requires open and honest discussion between the adoption agency, the fostering provider and the carer adopter, with advice from the agency medical adviser.

It will be necessary to be explicit about the nature of the concerns and to consider if there is any support that can be provided to reduce the perceived difficulties, risks or action required by the carer adopter. Where the health information leads to a decision not to proceed with the assessment, there should be discussion with the carer about whether this information should be shared with the fostering provider to address the issues raised and whether they impact on the carer continuing to foster. It is impossible to offer a definitive statement on how this situation should progress, as each scenario will be different. What is absolutely clear is that all stakeholders should be involved in discussions and a clear decision made in a timely way. Individuals must not be left drifting in a tide of uncertainty.

Impact on family members

When assessing prospective carer adopters who have birth children either living in the home or elsewhere, it is expected that the latter will be interviewed as part of the assessment process and that their views, wishes and feelings will be taken into consideration by the assessor. The differences between fostering and adoption must be clearly understood by all family members and any concerns should be addressed at an early stage. It is crucial that the lifelong nature of adoption is explored and that issues are considered from both a practical and emotional point of view.

For example, older birth children may have worries about sharing inheritance rights with an adopted sibling, or they might have anxieties about expectations that they will become responsible for the child should anything happen to the adoptive parent/s. Many of these issues will form part of the Stage Two assessment process but it is important that carers recognise that they are significant topics that will be covered with family members.

We would suggest that those family members who play an active part in the life of the foster family should be made aware that the carers wish to adopt the child. If grandparents, for example, have a particularly negative view of the child, this could impact on the stability of the placement and the self-esteem of the young person. Initial questions to be explored would be:

- Are the grandparents in favour of gaining another grandchild?

- What are their attitudes towards the child and the birth family?

- Is there any evidence of the child being treated differently?

It is important to examine these factors to gain a holistic picture of what life might be like for the adopted child in the future. It may be that the adoption agency can offer some guidance and support to relatives in this situation (see also 'Suggested reading for carer adopters' at the end of this guide).

Where it becomes evident later during the assessment that extended family members who may have been very supportive of a fostering arrangement are not in agreement with the plan for adoption, then workers will need to decide if this puts the proposal in jeopardy. Open and frank discussions are essential to prevent a possible future disruption. Where relatives or household members have objections or serious concerns but are not happy for these to be shared with the carer adopter applicants, then the agency must weigh up the risks attached to this course of action. We would suggest that every effort must be made by the agency to have these discussions openly and to encourage relatives to share their concerns with the applicants.

Where the carer adopter is involved in the care of other dependants, for example, a child with a significant disability or an elderly relative, then this too must be considered. The worker will want to explore whether the family's commitments may be too great in the future to ensure that the child in question will be prioritised. This may not be easy to measure but it should form part of the early discussion with the carer. This then provides an opportunity for the family to begin considering strategies that they can then explore in more detail.

Fahlberg comments that such situations should be thoroughly assessed and all parties should be consulted where possible. To inform decision making, it is crucial that the social workers involved have a clear picture of how the individuals regard the proposed adoption and how it is likely to impact upon them.

> *The social worker must not only assess the child's long term needs and the family's ability to meet those needs, but also the magical thinking of each member of the immediate family. What does adoption mean to the foster carers? Or to the child being adopted? Or to other members of the foster family? How do they expect it to change their relationships? Do the carers expect the child's behaviours or attitudes to change? Magical thinking about the effect of adoption is frequently prominent on the part of all involved.*
> Fahlberg, 2001, p1991

Space and physical conditions within the home

> *Children live in a foster home which provides adequate space, to a suitable standard.*

> *The foster home is warm, adequately furnished and decorated, is maintained to a good standard of cleanliness and hygiene and is in good order throughout. Outdoor spaces which are part of the premises are safe, secure and well maintained.*
> Standard 10 (10.2)
> National Minimum Standards for Fostering Service (NMS) 2011

All foster homes should meet the standards described above and should be routinely inspected by the supervising social worker as part of their visits. Where physical standards in the home are in question, this should have been a matter for their fostering service provider to address. If the home does not comply with Standard 10 of the NMS for Fostering Services, then it is unlikely that it will meet the standards required in adoption assessments.

Regulation 30(1) of the Adoption Agency Regulations 2005 (as amended) requires the adoption agency to obtain information about the prospective adopter which is specified in Part 3 of Schedule 4 as including 'information about the prospective adopter's home'. Statutory guidance does not cover the issue, but the Adoption National Minimum Standards 2011 offer a less detailed version of the fostering equivalent. Adoptive homes are expected to 'provide adequate space to a suitable standard' and:

9.1   The adoption agency ensures during the assessment of the prospective adopters' suitability to adopt, that the prospective adopters' home can comfortably accommodate all who live there. It is warm, adequately furnished and decorated, free of avoidable hazards, is maintained to a good standard of cleanliness and hygiene and is in good order throughout. Outdoor spaces which are part of the premises are safe, secure and well maintained.

9.2   The adoption agency has a written policy concerning safety for children in the prospective adopters' home, and in vehicles used to transport the child, which is regularly reviewed in line with the most recent guidance from relevant bodies.

This is something that must be addressed with the carer adopter at a very early stage. This can be a highly subjective area and it is important that the fostering service provider and adoption agency are both clear about what is an acceptable standard within the home and agree on how this is addressed. It should not come as a surprise to a foster family that their home is deemed "unsuitable" when they express an interest in adoption.

It is desirable that children being placed for adoption are able to have their own bedroom but it is not a legal requirement. Where a child in foster care has been sharing a bedroom with another child – possibly a sibling or the birth child of the foster carer – then it seems unreasonable for agencies to suggest that this situation cannot continue if the child is to be adopted, unless of course the children concerned are unhappy with the arrangement. It is important that carers are advised that the wishes and feelings of everyone in the family home will be sought as part of the discussions prior to assessment.

Where a very young child is sharing a bedroom with a foster carer, this is evidently not a situation that can continue as the child gets older, and if the foster carer has no other physical space then this must be discussed at the outset of any expression of interest in adopting the child. If a carer is able to move house or extend the property to accommodate the growing child, this might be seen as positive and a demonstration of their commitment to the child. On occasion, agencies may be able to provide the foster family with financial assistance for either a house move or property extension, but carers should not rely on this support.

Some agencies do have policies that require all looked after children to have their own bedroom and this must be discussed with families who may express an interest in adopting the child in their care. The main focus must be on the needs of the child both now and into the future and must take account of how these needs will be met.

Location

There are some geographical circumstances that may preclude a foster family from adopting the child in their care. These usually involve birth families who may know the child's current location or live in the vicinity who are known to be extremely dangerous or vexatious and who are assessed as likely to disrupt a permanent placement and/or pose a risk to the child. The risks in these situations must be considered at the outset and what may be relatively safe as a "temporary" arrangement, with birth family members accepting that the child is fostered, may become fraught with difficulty when adoption becomes the care plan. All adopters, including carer adopters, must be aware that it is almost impossible to guarantee complete anonymity and that they need to be realistic about the risks that they, their family and the child may be exposed to, and how they might manage these in the future.

However, it should also be recognised that in some situations the risks presented by birth parents may be minimal, and indeed they may be supportive of the foster carer adopting, so it is important that any risk assessment around geography takes account of the individual circumstances of the case.

If the risks are felt to be too great for the child remaining in the foster carer's current home in the longer term, then there needs to be open discussion about any options to move house/location. This may have implications for other children in the household, for example, a change of school, loss of friends, or for the carers themselves who may have to move further away from support networks. If the carers are willing to move then the agency will need to consider if they would offer any financial support towards the costs of moving.

One of the carer adopters who contributed to this guide commented:

> We had to change our names. I changed my surname and we had to change our youngest child's first name and surname...We had to move house and leave the borough we lived in and move 20 miles away. We received £1,700 towards removal costs.
> FCA 6

Another stated:

> It was decided by both the adoption team and P's social worker that I needed to move before they would consider me as a suitable adopter, due to his parents being aware of the town we lived in.

This is something that must be considered at an early stage in any discussions about the child's permanent care plan, and geographical issues should be clearly identified within the Child's Permanence Report (CPR).

Financial support and continuing to foster after adopting

In our consultation with foster carers who are either in the throes of adopting or who have adopted children whom they have looked after, it is clear from their responses that many of them faced a number of difficulties with this aspect of the process. The provision of financial support is often closely aligned to the question about whether a foster carer wants or is able to continue fostering once they have adopted. They may not have the physical space or emotional capacity to foster further children. Alternatively, it may be felt that it is not in the child's interests for the carers to continue to foster. Practice across agencies is extremely varied and there are a range of issues to be explored.

> So the time came to call the adoption team and put our interests in adoption forward. A meeting was held with the adoption team, social workers and our family. However, this is where our world felt like it had come crashing down. Without going into too much detail, we were told that if we wanted to go ahead any further we had to resign from fostering! This was my job, my career, my means of financially supporting my family. So, how would we be financially secure to care for an additional child and lose my job in order to adopt? We were devastated to feel so excluded, unfairly treated in comparison to other adopters who are not forced into giving up their jobs or careers. We were left with so many questions and unclear answers wherever we searched. It almost took over our everyday lives trying to find answers and solutions yet we could almost see the timer running out in front of our eyes. We encountered the most emotional rollercoaster! We were also told that we had to show we had funds to cover the next two years and that any financial support WOULD NOT be available.
> FCA 8

Many of the contributors to this guide made similar comments and this led us to consider what the "norm" is in these situations. We have considered this based on Regulations, Statutory Guidance, research evidence and "practice wisdom", and it would appear that the latter seems to be at the forefront of many agency decisions. A number of local authorities have policies that suggest that foster carers should cease fostering for a period which extends from the point of matching to the making of the adoption order, others referring to a predetermined period of time. Others are less prescriptive and recognise that where there are several children in placement, it is not appropriate to move children who are not part of the adoption plan whilst the carers go through the assessment and adoption process. Some agencies are pragmatic and recognise that they will need the ongoing services of the carer adopter in question.

The following comments were offered in April 2015 by adoption managers in two local authorities in Northern England.

> We ask the foster carer not to foster any new children until at least six months after the adoption order is granted.
> We offer a non-means-tested adoption allowance for the first two years of the placement. Thereafter it is means-tested. The allowance includes a contribution towards birthdays and Christmas. If the foster carers stop fostering altogether, they get the weekly payment for skills at their usual level for the first year; in Year Two it is level one payment for skills.
> LA manager 1

> In relation to taking time out of their fostering arrangements, this is dependent upon individual circumstances. There may be considerations where children have been in placement for a significant period and are very much part of the family unit and it would not be appropriate to disrupt this. There are times when we advise the need to take 6–12 months out, or it might be thought that fostering is no longer an option now the family has adopted. All of this is worked through with the family, fostering supervising social worker, the child's social worker and the adoption worker. It is far better to come to a joint agreement where everyone is happy.

> All foster carers have protected allowances for two years and will be means-tested thereafter. This is then reviewed on an annual basis. Foster carers are entitled to all post-adoption services and now have access to the Adoption Support Fund as a result, which can have a significant impact on therapeutic services for the family and child.
> LA manager 2

The discussion about whether or not it is in the child's best interests for the carers to continue fostering post-adoption is certainly one that should be had at the very beginning of the process and should take into account the financial implications for the family if they cease to foster.

In recent years, fostering has become more of a professional career choice for some families and the impact of reducing the family income needs to be measured. If the reality is that not only the adults but also the children will be significantly financially disadvantaged by them becoming an adoptive family, then consideration must be given to how this can be mitigated. This may mean a thorough exploration of benefits, any possible tax credits and what financial allowances can be provided by the local authority under Adoption Support Agency Regulations and for how long. Part of this will include consideration of a return to or the continuation of the fostering career and how this might be achieved. As shown by the following quotes, this can be a difficult area for discussion, but the provision of financial support needs to be resolved so that carers are aware of what will be on offer.

> *Our agency stated we could not foster for three years...[The local authority] continues to pay a fostering allowance for the three years so we are not affected financially.*
> FCA 6

> *They have agreed to meet my fostering allowance for two years as they have told me I cannot foster for the next two years. This does not help me pay for the extra rent for extra bedrooms I now have empty as I cannot foster.*
> FCA 5

> *I wanted to continue fostering. The adoption team wanted me to stop for at least three years. I did not see the need for this and financially was only happy to agree to two years when the two other long-term placements may have ended, otherwise I would have had to get a job and put her in childcare. In the end, I was allowed to foster again after one year as fostering were desperate – however, if the full three years had been insisted on it would have caused a major issue. I was also getting an adoption allowance for two years.*
> FCA 4

It is important for the carer adopters to be open about their financial circumstances at an early stage and to be clear about what benefits they may be entitled to should they require them post-approval and post-adoption; their social worker should help with this.

There appear to be two options open to the carer's fostering service provider: they can either recommend to the fostering panel that a carer's registration is terminated whilst the child is settling in, with a view to re-assessing the newly constituted family later on if required. Alternatively, they can put the foster carer "on hold" during this period with annual reviews that reflect this, convening a review of "significant changes in circumstance" when the carer is ready to return to fostering. In the former case, a carer may not agree with the agency recommendation to cease fostering and may seek a review with the IRM. It would seem sensible to work more collaboratively on this issue and ensure that all parties understand what is being proposed and are in agreement. If the carer is registered with an IFP, then the local authority may want to support the carer in these discussions.

We would suggest that to hold a definitive view on this matter could be detrimental to carer adopters and to the children and young people in placement. We would advocate that best practice would be to have a flexible approach that keeps children at the heart of the process, whilst ensuring that the carer adopter is not placed in an impossible financial position.

We recommend that a sensible approach is to consider each case on an individual basis, taking into account the assessed needs of all parties. This would require social workers completing an early and open assessment of the family situation and the needs of the child in question. Where the child is old enough, their views should also be sought during the main assessment.

Where it is assessed that a child requires a period of stability without other children leaving or joining the family, then the carer adopter needs to consider this at the outset. If a cessation of fostering means a significant drop in the family finances, thus impacting on the family's standard of living, then the fostering provider, adoption agency and children's service may need to consider what financial support can be provided under the Adoption Support Regulations 2005 to secure the permanent placement. Where a single foster carer or one of a couple is in employment, they should also consider whether they would be entitled to Statutory Adoption Pay and Leave.

In our discussions with carer adopters, we were also given examples of where they recognised the importance to the child of taking a break.

> *I love fostering and for myself would have probably liked to continue. However, we felt it best to take a break from fostering and to concentrate on being a "normal" family, settling into our new home and new life, etc. I hope to return to fostering one day, once our daughters are settled and if we feel they wouldn't be adversely affected.*
> FCA 6

> *There has been no pressure from their independent fostering agency – at present, they have decided they will review their commitment to fostering in one year and would include their adopted son in any decisions about this. Their fostering agency has said they can continue with training, etc, in the meantime. They would only consider offering respite placements in future. They do feel they have potential to offer help to other children once he feels secure.*
> FCA 11 via social worker

In some situations, it may be apparent that the child is extremely settled and well used to fostering and that the placement of other children has not had and will not have a negative impact. In cases where other children are already in placement with the child to be adopted, it is not recommended that these children are moved to facilitate the adoption process. Rather, children should be given age-appropriate explanations about their different care plans and these should be recorded as part of life story work for each child.

> *My adoption social worker was a wonderful woman, sensible, compassionate and insightful. Within a few meetings she had stated that she saw no reason for me to give up fostering. I already had another child in placement who had come while my son was living with his*

birth mother for that failed rehabilitation, and my son was used to him being around. My social worker felt it would be better for my son if we just started as we meant to go on, and that stopping fostering and then starting again would be more unsettling for him.
FCA 1

It is evident that, for foster carers wishing to pursue this course of action, it is most important that they are given early advice and guidance on what is required and what will be covered, and that fostering providers and adoption agencies have clear information to offer.

Current caregiving and parenting capacity

All adopter assessments focus on the applicant's suitability to adopt and their potential to parent via adoption. In each Prospective Adopter's Report (PAR), there is an expectation that evidence of skills, knowledge and experience will be apparent, and that an analysis of what has made the adopter the person they are will be central to the assessment. In the assessment of carer adopters this is no different and bears some discussion here. Much of the background information about the applicant may be found in their original fostering assessment, but what will make the PAR more robust and the assessment more thorough will be evidence of the foster carer's actual caregiving skills and attributes. The assessor can use examples of what the foster family has provided for children whom they have cared for and how their understanding of parenting children who have experienced neglect and trauma has developed since their initial approval. Information from annual foster carer reviews and child care reviews may be of help here and can be used in a way that does not identify the child by name. There should be many examples of good caring practice for this and other children that will aid the adoption panel and agency decision-maker when considering the carer adopter's suitability. There would also be the opportunity to obtain references from others involved with the child, for example, nursery workers, teachers, therapists and the fostering supervising social worker who can share their observations of the care provided and, for the match, also give evidence of the carers' understanding of and ability to meet the child's needs.

This is likely to be helpful where the carer adopters and children share different ethnic backgrounds. The assessment needs to explore the cultural competence of the adults and their capacity to promote and support the child's identity, and how they may manage these differences in the future. Do they appreciate that the young child may experience difficulties such as racism as they become older and be more aware of the reactions of others? How prepared are they to seek advice and guidance in the future?

A carer adopter's attitudes to contact with the child's birth family members is also worth exploring during this assessment. Have they been able to support direct contact, or has this been an area of difficulty? How do they feel about the child pursuing links with birth family as he or she gets older?

Where there are concerns or anxieties raised during the assessment about the current caregiver's standards of care or caring practices, these should be discussed with the fostering service so that they can also be considered as part of the ongoing fostering supervision and annual review process.

In our contributors' comments, it did appear that on occasion there were different standards applied by both adoption and fostering workers. One worker might interpret a household where routines were adhered to as "rigid", while another might see this as positive structure for a child, with clear boundaries. It is important that social workers can explore their own feelings about the style and quality of care that is being offered and also consider the risks and vulnerabilities of this as it relates to the particular child and their specific needs.

The summary of a carer adopter's PAR may look something like this:

Strengths

- **Previously adopted, parenting experience and experience of looked after children:** S and W have a wealth of proven experience caring for children, including some with special needs. They have raised birth children together and fostered many more over a 13-year period. Their own birth children are socially skilled, thoughtful and considerate young people who are clearly very attached to their family.

- **Stable and tested relationship:** the couple has been together for 20 years, facing difficulties together such as financial problems, bereavements, miscarriage and health difficulties. Their commitment to each other is evident and they operate very much as a team, each doing whatever needs to be done at the time, in what is inevitably a very busy household.

- The family has a lifestyle which is already child-centred.

- **Strong family support network:** the network is robust, tested and accessible and includes close family and friends, fostering peers and the post-adoption service and local authority.

- **Protective factors:** all of the children have expressed a wish for the family to adopt, having been well prepared and consulted. The children all have an existing relationship with each other and this has been observed and explored throughout the assessment.

- **The couple can accept different birth family experiences and life events:** they have established positive relationships with birth family members and demonstrate a capacity to engage in indirect and direct contact as appropriate.

- **Meeting an adopted child's individual needs:** fostering and adoption experiences demonstrate the couple's strengths in being adaptable and flexible in meeting a child's individual needs.

(Quoted with permission from a carer adopter's PAR where the child has significant health and emotional needs)

It would be unusual in any assessment not to find some areas of vulnerability and it is essential that these are addressed within the report. Panels often pick out such areas and request further exploration during the approval panel. By acknowledging these areas of potential concern within the PAR, the assessor should be able to reassure panel members. An example might be:

Vulnerabilities

- **High level of commitments:** the family does have a high level of commitments in their lives in terms of the couple's birth children. However, they ensure that all the children's needs are fully catered for and appear to thrive on the challenge of helping the children to achieve their full potential. They manage to have individual time together with the help of their support network.

(Quoted from a PAR)

PREPARATION OF CARER ADOPTERS

Chapter 3 of the Statutory Adoption Guidance 2013 (3.74) states that:

The agency should provide any necessary additional training, such as where the prospective adopters are seeking to adopt a child with needs that are very different to those of the child they have fostered/adopted.

It is expected that foster carers will have received a variety of training during their initial assessment process and subsequent to their approval. It is recognised that the type and amount of training is variable and that not all foster carers attend all the training available to them. Therefore, it is important that agencies are clear on what training has been completed by the carer, how this has impacted on their care practice and their knowledge and understanding of looked after children and young people. The carer training profile and personal development plan should be available in their annual Foster Carer Review and be considered as part of the assessment process. It is also important that agencies have a specific training programme or modules that are relevant to the needs of foster carers becoming adopters. This can be delivered in a group setting or with individual carers, and agencies can collaborate to provide this through a consortium or shared arrangement.

Suggestions for a course outline can be found below. This is based on a two-day course that was run by BAAF for the Yorkshire and Humber Adoption Consortia in 2012/13. The sessions ran from 10am till 2.30pm each day, giving time for carers to manage their child care duties. It is perfectly possible to adapt this to meet individual carer adopter needs and, if necessary, to deliver it on a one-to-one basis.

The topics covered, agreed with the agencies within the consortia, were:

- The lifelong nature of adoption
- Legal differences between fostering and adoption and the roles and responsibilities of the adoptive parent
- Child development and attachment
- Contact issues and managing issues with the birth family
- Behaviour management
- Education and health
- Talking about adoption and life story work
- Adoption support

The lifelong nature of adoption

In exploring this with carer adopters, it is important for them to be given an opportunity to consider and reflect on the massive commitment ahead and the expectations that they have of the child, themselves and others around them. Some of the issues that carer adopters may not have experienced as foster carers must be explored, along with what strategies they may need to develop. Talking openly and without prejudice about the child's history is significant. How much should be shared, when and with whom? As with any other adoption, the recommendation should be that children are always made aware that they are adopted and that they have ongoing access to age-appropriate life story materials. Carer adopters should be advised to speak sensitively about birth family members, but with honesty. Children should have access to factually correct information throughout their childhood.

Another issue raised in the feedback we received from carer adopters related to the lack of background information they had been given when the child was originally placed on a fostering basis. Training and preparation of carer adopters should emphasise that they should expect and ask for full background and health information and that, where possible, a Life Appreciation Day should be convened for the child. In the authors' experience as adoption panel chairs, carer adopters have commented that, despite knowing the child very well, the Life Appreciation Day has provided them with extra anecdotal information about birth family members and significant events of which they had previously been unaware. This extra information is important for carer adopters to be able to share as the child grows and matures.

Legal differences between fostering and adoption

It is important not to assume that carer adopters understand all the legal ramifications of becoming adopters, and preparation training should make these clear. One example might be to use Fahlberg's Three Aspects of Parenting (birth parent, legal parent and parenting parent) as a useful and graphic way of exploring these differences (2001, p149). This enables the applicants to consider how others in the family will understand the differences between fostering and adoption, and what strategies may have to be put in place to manage the needs of birth children or other foster children within the home. Fahlberg's work has been adapted by Nicholls in *The New Life Work Model* (2005) and this can be suggested as a helpful, child-friendly tool to use with children who may struggle with differences between fostering and adoption.

Child development and attachment

It is anticipated that most foster carers will, either during their Preparation to Care course or in subsequent fostering post-approval training, have spent considerable time exploring the impact of early trauma, separation and loss on child development. It is also anticipated that carers will have begun to understand the impact of interrupted development upon the child's attachment style and their capacity to make and sustain relationships. However, it is important for carer adopters to consider how the following concepts may impact on the way in which they become the permanent and legal parents to children, throughout not only their early years but adolescence and young adulthood.

- *Attachment formation*
- *Internal working models*
- *Mind-mindedness*
- *Attachment and resilience*

- *Impact of abuse and neglect*
- *Secure and insecure attachment patterns*
- *The importance of a secure base*

Schofield and Beek, 2014, p 4

Time could be spent on considering case examples and how the applicants can support the growing child in each of the domains identified below in the Secure Base Model. This can be a significant session as the carers start to focus on their specific child to whom they are making a commitment, rather than experiencing this as general training.

The Secure Base Model

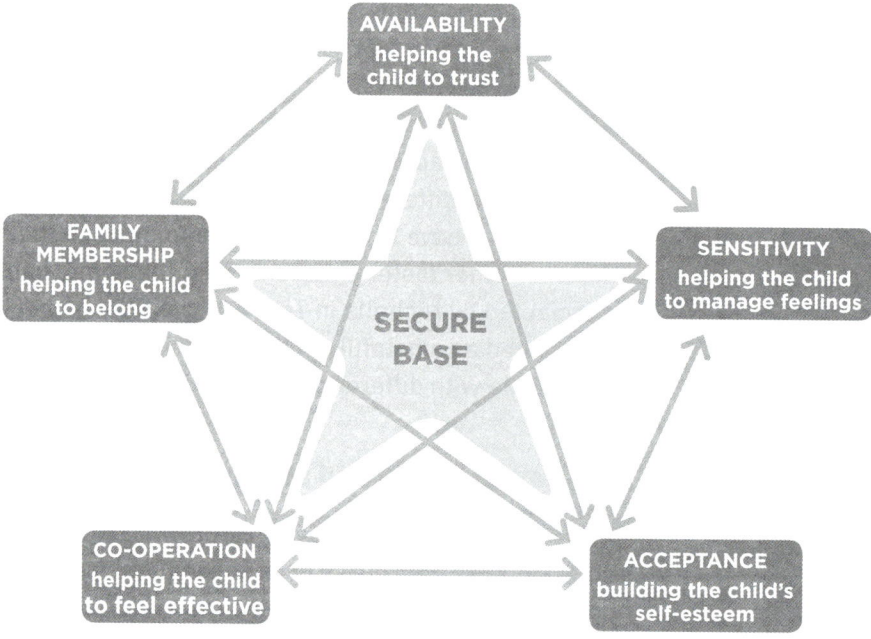

Schofield and Beek, 2014

Contact issues and the birth family post-adoption

I was told that I would have to move house to a location at least two boroughs away to provide a one-borough buffer between my family and the birth family...Over time, although social services still insisted that I move house (as the birth family knew where I lived), their restrictions as to location gradually relaxed until eventually, the new house I bought was only about half a mile from the old one, and actually just around the corner from the mainstay of my support network. I had said all along that as my son's birth family live in a far-flung corner of the borough, about as far away from me as they could be while still being officially in

the same borough, it was only necessary for me to change my address, not relocate to some distant place. It is highly unlikely, though not impossible, that I will ever see any of them on the street.
FCA 1

It is important to establish from applicants what contact arrangements they currently have in place and how these are managed – and how they might be managed should the child be adopted. Is direct contact something that the child wants and expects? Is this something that the carer adopters feel they can commit to? Are there any known "risk" factors? What are the benefits of contact and the problem areas? Who might support the child and the adopters if problems arise in the future?

Within this, the use of social media and its risks should be addressed and the concept of "anonymity" discussed. Advice about what photos are put on social media websites and the importance of privacy settings should be given. Emphasis on the fact that complete anonymity is impossible to achieve has to be included. Social media is an ever-changing medium and it is unhelpful to offer a definitive position on websites such as Facebook and Twitter.

As Fursland comments:

We can't tell right now, exactly where the revolution in social networking will take us or how adoption practice will change as a result. But one thing is certain – a new reality is emerging which will affect everyone touched by adoption.
2010, p 97

Behaviour management

This is a huge topic, as the age range of children who are adopted is quite varied, and some carer adopters will have accessed significant training as part of their fostering career, while others may be adopting the first child placed with them. Many of the carers who responded to us had adopted young children where there were gaps in the birth family history and therefore developmental uncertainties for the child. It is important that pointers are given to practical advice manuals and further post-approval training, with an emphasis on positive rather than punitive parenting. What must also be emphasised is that behaviour is a form of communication and that sensitive parenting can help children to manage their feelings, whatever their age. Prospective carer adopters should be encouraged to take advantage of training courses and support groups and be proactive in their search for guidance and support as their children grow and develop.

Useful and practical guidance can be found in *The Secure Base Model* (Schofield and Beek, 2014a), *Promoting Attachment and Resilience* (Schofield and Beek, 2014b), and *Reparenting the Child Who Hurts* (Archer and Gordon, 2013).

Education and health: the importance of having all the information

Practical advice should be given regarding obtaining health information about the child in placement. It has become evident that many carer adopters do not receive significant background information regarding the birth family of the child, sometimes until the adoption match is almost complete. Confidentiality is often quoted as the reason why such information is not shared. It should be made clear to prospective carer adopters that they should have *all* available information, as this may have implications for the child in the future. This guide advocates the use of Life Appreciation Days to assist with information sharing, even when the child has been in placement for some time. Of particular importance are any genetic or medical conditions affecting birth parents or siblings, the birth mother's use of alcohol during pregnancy, levels of domestic violence, substance misuse and neglectful parenting. As adoption panel Chairs, we have received comments in matching panels from carer adopters that Life Appreciation Days have been of great benefit in filling in gaps in their knowledge about birth family members and the child's early history and experience (see Sayers and Roach, 2011).

Also of significance is information about the education of the birth family. Did they attend school? Did they go to university or obtain a technical qualification? Were there any academic successes? Were there any known learning needs or difficulties? Again, this information is sometimes not shared and could have implications for the child and the expectations that others have of that child.

Carer adopters should receive information about post-adoption support in education, such as the availability of the Pupil Premium in England.

Talking about adoption and life story work

Children separated from their birth families need honest information about and explanation for their life changes immediately the separation takes place.
Nicholls, 2005, p 30

The telling process isn't just about telling a child they are adopted, it's about giving them information and explanation. It's called a process because it never is a one-off task, it changes and evolves as a child grows into maturity.
Nicholls, 2005, p 172

Carer adopters must be aware that, as adoptive parents, they should be able to share the child's birth story and origins with their child throughout his or her childhood. Where a child has been with a carer for some time, there may have been a temptation to gloss over the child's early life experiences or to not speak about their birth family. Carer adopters should be advised during their preparation that the adopted child has a right to information about their birth family, the decisions made by the agency, and the reasons why they were placed with and adopted by the carer adopters. It is recognised that when a child is placed in foster care, some families are not given full background information about them, or can feel constrained by ongoing court proceedings and parental contact, and that this means they cannot talk fully and frankly with the child. Once the plan to adopt is made, the carer must have access to the same information that any other adopter would have, and must consider how they will share this with the child now and in the future.

It is anticipated that carer adopters will be given advice and guidance about doing life story work with the child and using information contained in the CPR to assist the child as their curiosity grows. During one of the training sessions run by BAAF, a carer adopter gave a positive example of how they had started a later life letter for the child and in it had explained how the family had felt on the arrival of the child and that gradually the whole family had come to love them.

Adoption support

Carer adopters should be given information about what adoption support they may be entitled to seek and how they can ask for help. They should be given access to information about the local adoption support service and details of how and when they can call on them for help. Chapter 5 covers adoption support in more detail, outlining matters that are specific to carer adopter applications.

THE PANEL

Once the preparation and assessment is complete and the applicants have had an opportunity to read the PAR (making amendments if necessary), the case will be presented to the adoption panel. As in all other adoption and fostering cases, applicants must be invited to attend. There is no obligation to attend, but it is acknowledged good practice.

Applicants should be thoroughly prepared for the panel meeting and briefed in how the particular agency manages the adoption panel. They should be clear that the approval panel is to consider their suitability to adopt and that the matching panel will follow this. Many agencies timetable both cases on the same panel day.

The panel...asked us quite a few questions but I felt they were just piecing the jigsaw together and getting a full picture of us as a family to make sure this was the right decision for us all.
FCA 14

[Panel was] like a friendly inquisition. Due to the report, I prepared very well for the panel and all areas of the report. I was concerned to ensure that I had detailed answers such as about [the child's] dual heritage (my nieces are dual heritage and are positive role models), also my own childhood – my parents fostered several children of black African heritage in the late 1960s.
FCA 7

I completed the same assessment process as any other adopter, complete with adoption preparation training. The home study was perhaps a little shorter than others as social services already had much information from the fostering approval. Panel covered approval and matching on the same day. From initial enquiry to panel took just under 10 months. I found the whole process excellent, including panel, which was an encouraging and upbuilding experience. This was, in large part, due to my excellent social worker who I can't praise highly enough... There were no questions to answer at panel, and every single panel member said that they were delighted with this outcome.
FCA 1

KEY POINTS

- Ensure that there is a robust agency policy and procedure relating to carer applications to adopt that is easily accessible to fostering services, the adoption team child care workers, and IROs.

- Provision of joint staff training that enables childcare services to develop a consistent approach in these cases will be helpful.

- Provision of a clear practice guide that can be given to carers who are contemplating expressing an interest in adopting the child in their care will also be of use.

- It is good practice to have an early viability discussion with foster carers that is open and transparent and gives clarity about the significant differences between temporary foster care and the legally binding lifelong nature of adoption. This discussion should be fully recorded.

- Specific preparation for foster carers adopting should be provided, preferably within a group setting, but if not, then delivered on a one-to-one basis, with an opportunity to talk with other carer adopters.

Chapter 4
The matching process

Linking refers to the process of investigating the suitability of one or more prospective adoptive families who might meet the needs of a certain child or sibling group based on their Prospective Adopter Reports (PAR). Matching refers to the process wherby a local authority decides which prospective adoptive family is the most suitable to adopt a particular child.
Dance *et al*, 2010, p 1

What do we know about linking and matching children who are already in placement? In many ways, it would appear to be an excellent placement choice that means children avoid the separation and loss issues associated with moving placement. The link relies on actual evidence of practical caregiving rather than the rather unscientific processes associated with profiling children and family finding. Surprisingly though, matching children with their current foster carers as adopters appears to be a taxing process for many social work practitioners and, according to some of the carers in our survey, quite a frustrating and long-winded one.

In any matching process, it is of crucial importance to have as much information as possible about both the child and the prospective adopters. In the latter case, the adopter's characteristics, such as their parenting styles and skills, and their extended family and support networks should be a consideration along with their understanding, attitudes to and expectations of adoption. Their appreciation and understanding of the child's history and any ongoing contact arrangements must be measured. In addition to this, Dance *et al* highlight the importance of 'chemistry – or a feeling of emotional connectedness with a particular child' (2010, p 5). This confirms much anecdotal evidence from adoption panels. When prospective adopters are asked why they feel that this child is right for them, they frequently make comments such as: 'He looks like XXX in our family'; 'We fell in love with her cheeky smile'; 'She loves the same things as me'; 'He is a really busy character, just like me'.

In the case of carer adopters, the "chemistry" is very often the most significant driver, and is based on actually living together rather than vaguer notions of a child's personality based on limited information. Carer adopters will have an existing relationship with a child whom they have gradually got to know, and have begun to "claim" that child emotionally and physically. Comments such as: 'We could not imagine her moving away from our family'; 'He is so settled with us and fits right in with extended family'; 'She calls me Mummy and that feels right' are not unusual. FCA 13 comments that: 'R naturally became part of our family and wanted by us all'.

Given the wealth of information that should be readily available in carer adopter applications, the documentation relating to matches between the child and their carer is sometimes superficial and poor.

Regulations set out that once the match is identified as being appropriate, an Adoption Placement Report (APR) and Adoption Support Plan (ASP) will be presented to the agency adoption panel, along with the updated Child Permanence Report (CPR) and the Prospective Adopter's Report (PAR). CoramBAAF has recently published a new Adoption Placement Plan form and an APR that incorporates the ASP. This APR also incorporates a Matching Grid and Parental Responsibility form and these should assist workers in focusing more effectively on the link.

Adoption panels frequently report that the paperwork does not help them to understand the rationale of the proposed placement, particularly where the prospective carer adopter does not appear to meet all of the child's identified needs.

This chapter considers some of the significant areas associated with linking and matching and how they relate specifically to foster carers planning to adopt.

IMPORTANCE OF HAVING FULL INFORMATION

In carer adopter applications, it is anticipated that the foster family will, through living with the child, have a huge amount of information about them. However, this should not be assumed and it may be that significant information has not been shared, particularly about the child's birth family. Good practice requires that an up-to-date and full assessment has been completed relating to the child. This requires updating the CPR and might include a Life Appreciation Day. It must be clear what health needs the child currently has and if there are any background factors that might impact on this into the future; the birth mother's use of alcohol during pregnancy would be one of these factors. Parental mental ill health, learning disability, domestic violence, physical health conditions and early trauma, abuse and neglect would also require careful consideration as they may have a later impact on the child.

Looked after children have poor outcomes in many areas of health and social functioning: mental health is a particular issue. Comprehensive initial assessments are absolutely key to understanding the current and future health needs of looked after children and in providing them and their carers with the information they need to keep healthy in future years.
Burton, 2015, p 43

Often, carer adopters express concerns that the placing agency has not shared aspects of birth family members' health history due to Data Protection restrictions.

If a parent refuses to consent to sharing their own medical records, it may still be possible to obtain relevant information. Information held on the mother's records may also be the child's information, to which they would be entitled under Data Protection Act principles, so, for example, a mother may refuse to allow disclosure about her substance use during pregnancy, but the information that the foetus failed to gain an appropriate birth weight because of maternal smoking is the child's information and so can be shared.
Conroy Harris and Bracewell, 2015, p 92

Where an agency intends to pursue the carer adopter's application, it is essential that all efforts are made to obtain consent to share information prior to the matching panel. Carer adopters who are unaware of the child's birth family health history remain at a disadvantage throughout the child's life. If birth parents can be made aware that it is the foster carer adopting the child and so support the placement, this may increase the likelihood of them being prepared to share their information.

USING EVIDENCE FROM HOW THE CARER ADOPTER ALREADY MEETS THE CHILD'S NEEDS

Throughout the adoption assessment of the carer adopter, the evidence of their ability to meet a child's needs should have been actively considered. Within the APR, more specific examples of how they will promote *this* child's particular needs will be required, and because a foster carer/adopter has already been doing this, evidence should be readily available from a range of documents including the child care review process, foster carer supervision and the foster carer review process.

For example, in relation to health, there should be evidence that appointments have been kept and that the carer adopters have been mindful of the child's physical and emotional well-being. The same might be true about behavioural and educational issues. Has the carer adopter supported the child in school? What have they done to help the child overcome any difficulties? This can all be provided as evidence within the matching report.

RACE AND ETHNICITY

Draft Statutory Adoption Guidance 2014 (DfE, 2014a) sets out that:

3.4 A prospective adopter can be matched with a child with whom they do not share the same ethnicity, if they can respect, reflect or actively develop a child's racial identity from the point they are matched and as they develop throughout their childhood.

3.8 What matters in the matching of a child with a prospective adopter of differing ethnicity are the qualities, experiences and attributes the prospective adopter can draw on and their level of understanding of how discrimination and racism operate in society at both an individual and institutional level.

Where the child and the prospective adopters do not share a similar racial or ethnic background, it must be considered in the APR how the adults recognise the child's ethnic and cultural needs and what attempts have been made to incorporate aspects of these into daily living. For carer adopters, it should be easier to do this than with "stranger" adopters, as there is the lived experience of that child within that family to draw on. The APR has a section on identity and it is important that all aspects of this are explored, and that there is specific analysis of how this child's identity needs are being met now and how this might continue into the future. So the PAR will likely contain general information about attitudes to identity and diversity, and the APR will be about the specific child.

> *She is insightful in how working in different diverse communities have shaped her to be the person she is today and is able to not only embrace diversity and other cultures, but she practises being part of different communities and exploring new cultures during her daily life...it is part of who she is.*
> (Quote from a PAR)

We deliberately live in a mixed community. It is a wonderful blend of elderly folk and young families, many ethnicities and cultures. Each year we help run a street party to which many neighbours come and showcase their cultures with food, beautiful clothes and party games...so that [the child] will naturally experience inclusivity and that we value and welcome difference.
Adopter quoted in an APR,
used with the permission of a carer adopter and Sheffield City Council

ASSESSING ATTACHMENT IN THE CONTEXT OF EXISTING RELATIONSHIPS

With carer adopters, it should be easier to assess how attachment issues might play out, given that the child is already in placement and there is no need to, for example, predict how they might adjust to a move to "stranger" adopters, or how a new home might trigger feelings and behaviours that are currently not fully evident.

Cairns (2002) offers some useful guidance for practitioners that might be helpful in exploring the carer adopter's understanding of the particular child's emotional needs and how they manage these on a day-to-day basis. Within the APR, this evidence can be provided to assist the reader in understanding the strength of the placement into the future.

- Does the carer adopter recognise that the child's behaviour is a form of communication and is this managed in a mostly appropriate way?

- Does the carer adopter have a playful and curious approach to the child's behaviour or is it a more punitive approach?

- How does the carer adopter manage any behavioural issues exhibited by the child?

The assessment of the relationship between the adults and the child is essentially a way of predicting how the family will function in the future and it is therefore important for workers to observe and analyse how current challenges are managed. The exploration of these issues should then assist in developing a more robust support plan.

Linking and matching in any adoption requires that all the above issues are considered. In a situation where the child is already living with the family, the worker will be fortunate enough to be able to observe how the family dynamics are played out and to incorporate evidence within the PAR, the CPR and APR. Where there are significant concerns that the carer does not appear to understand the child's attachment needs and is "out of kilter" with the child, this must be addressed at a very early stage in the process. It is vital that where there are such concerns, the worker is open with the carer about this, and the agency offers training and support to try and aid the carer's personal development.

It is not unusual that children displaying avoidant, ambivalent or disorganised patterns of attachment can be challenging to care for at times. What is important in the carer adopter assessment and matching process is that these challenges are acknowledged and there is evidence of how the carer adopter manages and plans strategies to mitigate against disruption of the placement. This also ties in to the plan for adoption support: what is being provided to ensure that the family remains resilient enough to deal with the child's growth into adolescence and adulthood?

FAMILY AND SOCIAL RELATIONSHIPS

Parenting is a highly subjective concept and varies considerably across continents and cultures. Adults as well as children have tendencies to behave in ways that they have learned from previous situations. We are all impacted upon by our early life experiences, our relationships with others and life in general. The internal working model of the carer adopter is therefore significant when caring or parenting by adoption. It is hoped that throughout the initial fostering assessment process and the ongoing supervision, support and review of the foster carer, the agency would have a view about the parenting style of the carer and that this can be shared and discussed between fostering and adoption services in a constructive and transparent manner. Much of this should be considered throughout the Stage Two adoption assessment.

At the matching stage, the more general evidence and analysis of "parenting style and capacity" discussed in the PAR needs to be related very much to how the carer adopter's family and social relationships have the potential to meet *this* child's ongoing needs throughout the child's life.

- Is the carer adopter physically and emotionally available to the child currently and likely to be into the future? Is the carer adopter able to "stand in the child's shoes"?

- Has the carer adopter demonstrated a reflective and flexible approach, showing that they can share their own feelings with the child in a sensitive way?

- Is the carer adopter able to show the child that they are unconditionally valued for who they are, for their difficulties as well as their strengths?

- Does the carer adopter actively promote the child's autonomy, working collaboratively and co-operatively with the child to develop confidence?

- Does the carer adopter include the child in all aspects of family life, whilst acknowledging that the child does have a background history and a birth family?

(Adapted from Schofield and Beek, 2006)

In considering these elements, the social workers should be able to provide a clear and evidential analysis of the reasons why this child should remain with this carer and how the carer adopter will be able to meet the identified specific needs of that child on a permanent basis.

PAPERWORK AND ADOPTION PANEL

As in any adoption match, the completed assessments (PAR and CPR, including up-to-date health, education and therapeutic information) must be presented to the adoption panel alongside the APR and ASP. These documents must be signed by all parties and it is expected that they will be proofread and quality assured prior to distribution.

Although not a legal requirement, it is best practice that carer adopters should be invited to attend the panel and should have received the paperwork at least 10 days prior to the meeting so that they can make amendments or additions. They should also be prepared for the panel process. Panels do vary and the carers should be given full information about who is on the panel, what form the meeting will take and what is expected of them.

The PAR should incorporate all factual information about the applicants and the reasons for their decision to pursue adoption for this child. The PAR should concentrate on evidence of skills and capacity and should also address any vulnerabilities as well as identify strengths. This report is all about suitability to adopt and the assessor must focus on all issues identified in Chapter 3 of this guide.

The APR/ASP is designed to be a collaborative effort between adoption and child care social workers and the carer adopter themselves. The reader must be left in no doubt as to the recommendation and should understand how and why *this* family can meet the needs of *this* child on a lifelong basis. It is expected that where the carer adopter has some difficulty in putting pen to paper, the workers will support and guide them to ensure that their voices are heard. Where the child is of sufficient age and understanding, it is expected that their wishes and feelings will be fully evident in the paperwork (both the CPR and APR).

The child stated in a letter that he had written to the judge in the court proceedings: 'I am 100 per cent sure that I would like to be adopted by "this family" because they do what's best.'
Quote from an eight-year-old dual heritage boy. The panel was also presented with some handwritten documents and drawings that made his wishes and feelings very clear, FCA 13

In terms of adoption support, the paperwork must identify the current needs of the child and how these are being addressed. Will the child remain eligible for therapeutic support once they become an adopted child? Who will pay for this and for how long? It must also address the needs of the carer adopters. If they are recieving extra allowances for the child, for instance, if they are particularly destructive, how will this be addressed when their status changes from looked after to adopted?

These questions are considered in more depth in the next chapter, but applicants and social workers need to have a clear picture of what is on offer at the time of the matching panel.

PLACEMENT AND REVIEW

Following the panel and agency decision, if all is agreed, the child then becomes subject to Adoption Agency Regulations and the placement becomes an adoptive placement rather than a fostering placement. The child remains subject to looked after (LAC) reviews till the adoption order is granted. It is anticipated that the carer adopter will submit their application to the court to adopt as soon as they feel comfortable doing so. Because it is likely that the child will have been in a continuous placement with them for over 10 weeks, there is no requirement for the carer adopter to wait to lodge their application. It is usual for this application to be lodged following the first review as an adoptive placement. The Annex A report for court can be completed using much of the information in the CPR, PAR and APR – see Appendix 3.

It was a fantastic, enjoyable day on which we made the little boy feel really special by attending court in a limo, having a family meal in which the child's social worker was included, and then hired a children's play centre for all the children. The judge was even impressed with how many attended for the special celebration and we will make sure it's a very special event again next time.
FCA 14

KEY POINTS

- Ensure that carer adopters have access to full information relating to the child and their birth family; a Life Appreciation Day is highly recommended.

- Ensure that the matching process considers the attachment style of both adult and child: how are they working together?

- Local authorities should provide a comprehensive guide for social workers completing the matching paperwork (APR and ASP) and ensure that the paperwork is throughly quality assured prior to being sent to the adoption panel.

- Workers must present analytical and evidential reports that have been checked, proofread and signed.

- Ensure that all parties are fully prepared for attending the adoption panel.

Chapter 5
Adoption support

When foster carers adopt the children in their care through an agency adoption, their entitlement to adoption support services will be the same as for all other adopters.

They should have access to advice and information, counselling, support groups for adopters and adopted children, support for contact, dealing with health or education issues and any other concerns affecting the adoption placement, financial support and access to therapeutic services.

If they continue to foster, they will also be able to access training and support groups in their fostering role.

Research has shown that some of the reservations expressed by foster carers about adopting relate to their concerns about the different levels of support available to adopted children, compared to the support available to fostered children. Recent changes have addressed some of these issues, particularly in relation to education, and carer adopters should be made aware of these.

The carer adopter should receive a copy of the Adoption Passport,* which was introduced to meet the requirements of s.6 of the Children and Families Act 2014 to provide information on adoption support services so that adopters are aware of their entitlements.

One of the advantages of foster carers adopting is that as the child is remaining with their current carers, there should already be a good understanding of the child's needs through the assessments completed by their social worker, during care proceedings, and through their adoption medical, and that the child and their adoptive parents can continue to access support that is already in place in relation to their health, education and emotional needs.

> She has always received a lot of support from her family and friends and they are a very close knit group. She did contact the Children with Disability Team when she was unsatisfied with the support B was being offered at school. This was a time when she was glad B had been known to social services as she was able to have the support of the team.
> FCA 10 via social worker

---

* See www.first4adoption.org.uk/wp-content/uploads/2014/07/The-Adoption-Passport.pdf

ACCESSING ADOPTION SUPPORT

When the child is being matched with their foster carers, their social worker should have prepared a detailed adoption support plan outlining the child's assessed current and predicted needs and the type of support the carer adopters will require to parent the child. This plan is presented to the matching panel and should be discussed and reviewed at childcare reviews held prior to the adoption order being made, so that the carer adopters know how to access help and support in the future. The plan will also provide reassurance to carer adopters that support will still be available to them.

There was evidence from some of those carer adopters who shared their stories with us that this had not always been the case in the past.

> *Our discussions about post-adoption support were rather brief and vague. My son presents with no obvious concerns – he was, and still is, meeting milestones, has no evident health concerns and has the advantage of being with me since a very early age. In retrospect, though, I think I was quite naive in this area. Speaking to other adopters, I now realise that most adopters put a lot more thought into the whole thing before they even apply, whereas my decision was a lot more spontaneous! Other adopters I have met have read lots of books and done lots of research, and so have come to the post-adoption support conversation much more clued up than I was. I don't think I had thought enough about what support my son and I might conceivably need in the future and was happy enough to go along with a fairly vaguely-worded statement about availability of support based on the fact that, at the time, my son seemed to have no particular needs. Things are still going well, so it hasn't become an issue. I don't know what exactly will happen should I need such support in the future, but I do know who to call!*
> FCA 1

> *Once the assessment was underway, we were briefly told by the child's Independent Reviewing Officer about assessments which can be made to determine the level of support both financially and for other needs. However, we were also told by the adoption team that because our child had no additional needs we wouldn't be required to undertake the assessment.*
> FCA 8

It is important that carer adopters understand that at any point after the adoption order has been made, they can apply to the placing local authority for support services and, where necessary, that this will include having an assessment of their support needs as set out in the Adoption Support Regulations 2005.

For carer adopters who are not living in the local authority's area, they should be made aware that adoption support will be provided by the placing authority for the first three years after adoption but that it will then become the responsibility of the local authority where they live. It is possible to explore with that local authority what adopter support services they offer that the carer adopter could therefore access, e.g. newsletters, training or support groups. The exceptions to this will be any agreements about ongoing financial support and existing contact arrangements.

Where the carer adopters are continuing to foster, it will be important that their supervising social worker refers them to the adoption service to access the relevant support if issues arise relating to the adopted child and can, if needed, support them in doing this if necessary, e.g. if there were previous tensions around the adoption.

ACCESSING THERAPEUTIC SUPPORT

The introduction of the Adoption Support Fund* (ASF) in England in 2015 meant that where therapeutic needs were identified within the adoption support assessment and subsequent plan, the local authority should apply to the ASF and funding would be agreed before the adoption order was made. In 2016, the Government changed the parameters so that therapeutic support could commence before the adoption order was made. The ASF is available for children and young people, up to and including the age of 18 or up to 25 if they have a SEN Statement/EHC Plan, or who have been adopted from local authority care in England or who were adopted from Wales, Scotland or Northern Ireland more than three years ago but are living in England.

Some of the carers we heard from, who are currently in the process of adopting their child, were aware of the ASF and what therapeutic support was being lined up for their child post-adoption.

Many local authorities will look first at therapeutic input being provided by their local CAMHS, with some having special arrangements in place for their looked after children. However, this provision does not always extend to adopted children and it will be important that carer adopters are given clear information about local resources and how to access them. They may have previously had consultations with CAMHS, which will often extend this facility to foster carers rather than undertaking direct work with children whilst they are in temporary care. Where the social work assessment has identified that the child has therapeutic needs relating to emotional, behavioural or attachment difficulties, it is worth considering whether an early referral could be made to CAMHS or the ASF as part of the adoption support plan, for work to commence once the adoption placement has been confirmed.

---

*   See www.adoptionsupportfund.co.uk.

FINANCIAL SUPPORT

Financial support was discussed earlier in this book as an important point to consider before assessment and matching takes place. Where an ongoing financial allowance has been agreed, carers need to understand whether some parts of that will be means-tested on an annual basis and how these reviews will be conducted. For some local authorities, this is a basic administrative process, while others use it as an opportunity to contact adoptive families and discuss whether any support is needed. The financial arrangements agreed should be clearly set out in the Adoption Support Plan and, where necessary, as a written agreement, including the arrangements for review.

Many local authorities offer some form of additional financial support to carer adopters for the first two years after the order has been made. This is often linked to the expectations around their ongoing role as a foster carer. In specific cases, sometimes local authorities will agree to a continuation of financial payments equivalent to the fostering allowances or fees until the child is 18, where this is seen as securing the adoption placement. Again, it is important to be clear about any means testing or review requirements around this.

Financial support may also be made available to facilitate ongoing direct contact arrangements with the child's family members or siblings.

Carer adopters should be aware that they can request financial support after adoption as part of any ongoing assessment of their support needs.

SUPPORT FOR ADOPTERS

Carer adopters should be added to the local authority's mailing list and invited to any adoption support groups and training events organised by the local authority. There should also be some thought given to how they can continue to retain the support they currently have from other foster carers if they are not continuing to foster either in the short or longer term, for example, can they still access foster carer training or support groups? They may not feel that they "fit in" at adoption support groups, but might benefit from being linked up or "buddied" with other foster carers who have adopted, or with adoptive parents. Some may have retained contact with the adopters of children they previously fostered, who may now form part of their support group.

Feedback from some of the carer adopters who responded to us showed that some of them were accessing training events or adoption support groups being run by their local authority or other agencies such as

Adoption UK. The example below also illustrates the importance of carers' informal networks for them.

> *We have a wide circle of fostering friends, some of whom have also adopted, and that is where the majority of our support comes from. We are also close friends with some of the families of children we moved on to adoption. They are available to talk to regarding letterbox, contact with siblings, how to discuss the child's life story, etc. I have not received, and nor have I requested any post-adoption support. I have a large support network through the church I have attended for over 20 years, including a couple of other families who foster or have children on a residence order. I did attend a free training course entitled Adoption: What to Tell and When.*
> FCA 1

The following example also shows the flexible approach being taken by an IFP to allow a carer adopter to still access foster carer training whilst "on hold".

> *Their fostering agency has said they can continue with training (while they decide whether they will continue to offer respite fostering in the future.)*
> FCA 11 via social worker

As has been described earlier in this guide, a number of the carer adopters who contacted us felt that they had to fight to be able to adopt their children. Unfortunately, as a result this has left some of them reluctant to ask social workers for support. Although they do not identify particular areas at present where they need support, we know that adoption support can be more effective if it is being offered at an earlier stage rather than at a time of crisis or longstanding difficulties. Where there are separate adoption support workers or teams, it may be helpful to introduce carer adopters to these services prior to adoption to encourage their engagement.

> *I was promised help from a social worker who has not contacted us since the adoption. I have been included in the support groups but again only after several requests. After being treated the way we were, we don't feel able to request anything from the adoption team!*
> FCA 2

> *I would go to other carers and adopters as I no longer have any trust in social services.*
> FCA 5

Although there has been some discussion about enabling adopters who have lost trust in their local authority to access services from the ASF through another local authority or adoption agency, at the time of writing this has not been put in place. However, it is possible for local authorities to commission adoption support assessments through an adoption support agency or independent adoption support agency worker to inform their decisions about making an application to the fund.

Other carer adopters were clear about the need to access support when they needed it.

> *All of my support currently comes from family and friends. Mostly friends actually, as my family live abroad, although they help where they can. However, this is because, up to this point, I have not considered that we need professional support. Should things change, I would certainly seek professional input.*
> FCA 1

SUPPORT IN EDUCATION

If the child is due to start school or a decision is being made to change schools (perhaps to move the child to a more local school), their carer adopters need to be made aware that all children adopted from care can receive priority access to schools.* Also, where they have adopted a younger child, they should be made aware of access to free school places for two-year-olds.

The child will continue to be eligible for the Pupil Premium or Early Years Pupil Premium,† and although the requirement for PEP meetings will end once they are adopted, it will be important in the time leading up to the adoption going through to discuss how any support already in place will be continued. This information should also be included in the Adoption Support Plan.

Carer adopters should be made aware of the need to inform any new school or nursery of their child's adoptive status to ensure that the school claims the Pupil Premium and their child receives direct benefit from it.

For some children and their carer adopters, the continuity of remaining at their school where they are known, where support is already in place and where there are already good working relationships will be a distinct advantage.

> *His school have been very supportive – he's been there for six years. He is very happy there and his progress is exceeding their expectations.*
> FCA 11

---

*   See https://www.gov.uk/government/publications/school-admissions-code--2.

†   Further information on the Pupil Premium is available from a question-and-answer document from the DfE (www.baaf.org.uk/webfm_send/3813) and a BAAF report: *Pupil Premium for Adopted Children: Case studies* (www.baaf.org.uk/webfm_send/3879).

School and nursery have been very supportive. Our eldest daughter needed support prior to the adoption but hasn't needed it since. Her school are supportive.
FCA 6

However, some carer adopters may also need some support or encouragement in assuming the parental responsibility that will be gradually handed over to them once the child is formally placed through to the adoption order being made. The extent to which they were enabled to make decisions through delegated authority as a foster carer will vary depending on the practice of the local authority and whether they were part of an in-house or external provider, and they may need to adjust to their new role with regards to their child's education.

Carer adopters should be aware that they can seek support from adoption services in managing any issues that emerge for their child in school or other education settings. Adoption support workers are familiar with the need to help adopters advocate for their child to obtain additional support, to negotiate assessments for special educational needs or to provide additional insight to school staff about the difficulties a child may have as a result of their previous experiences.

LIFE STORY WORK

It is likely that some carer adopters will have known their child for much of their lives or at least their life since entering care; indeed, some of those who provided comments had collected their child from hospital, had been their only foster placement and, in one case, had been there at the birth. For other carer adopters, their child may have experienced a number of placements or life experiences before coming into their care.

Life story work and books for both younger and older children are still an important tool for the carer adopters in helping their child understand their past. Although these carers will be able to provide the photos and mementos they have gathered since the child joined their family, they will be reliant on social workers for the photos and materials that will help the child understand their early life experiences. It may be that where there are positive relationships between birth family members and the carer adopter, they could be more successful in obtaining information and mementos for the child than a social worker. However, it will also be important for the worker preparing a book or completing work with an older child to work jointly with the carer so their involvement with the child, and in some cases the child's parent or parents, during the period of fostering can be captured as part of the information bridging from the child's past to their future.

Where the foster carer is adopting an older child with a more complex history, a Life Appreciation Day should be considered, and where there is an identified need for more therapeutic life story work, an application for funding can be made to the ASF.

SUPPORT FOR CONTACT

Post-adoption contact for children adopted by their carer should be considered on an individual basis, based on their particular situation.

Whilst many agencies have established practice (and sometimes policies) about what contact arrangements should be put in place following adoption, in some cases existing relationships between the carer adopters and birth family members or the carers of other siblings may mean they are more open about the type of contact they are prepared to consider.

> *The success of a contact plan depends on the qualities of mutual understanding that the adults can bring to it...Contact works best when it happens through collaboration, when the adopters have been fully briefed about the birth family's history, and hopefully have met the birth parents, and can take ownership of the contact arrangements that are agreed between them and all the other parties, and can play a full part in ensuring the arrangements are wholly focused on the child's needs.*
> Schofield and Beek, 2006

When planning and agreeing contact arrangements post-adoption, it is important that the views of the carer adopters and, where appropriate, the child are considered. Whilst the following examples may not be seen as usual practice, they are supported by the findings of the Contact after Adoption study (Neil *et al*, 2015) where it was noted that:

> *An open and empathic attitude on the part of adoptive parents was the factor most closely related to whether or not contact continued or increased and the satisfaction of all parties with the arrangements.*
> p 15

> [The birth mother] *did assume that we would allow her to continue to see her daughter. We have arranged for the baby to see her birth mother and maternal grandmother every four months. This was decided solely by us and it is arranged by us and the birth mother. It is going very well at the moment and the birth family is very respectful of our feelings and appreciative. We hope that this contact will be beneficial for our daughter and help her to know her story.*
> FCA 2

I know that while the birth mother and grandmother were not happy about the idea of adoption, they were happy that if she was being adopted it was by me, as they did know that I would care for her. Once a year direct contact with the birth mother and birth grandmother was decided by the guardian – she wanted the birth grandmother to have contact and I said I would only agree if the birth mother was included, as I did not think it was fair to her or the child.

I recently discovered that [birth mother] wanted to add great grandma into contact and thought I would be fine with it. As my child has no relationship with her, having not seen her for over two years, I have said no and think they were surprised by this.
FCA 4

It is important to take account of birth parents' views, but also to be clear about the boundaries and arrangements that are to be put in place, as illustrated below. Birth parents who have previously had phone or text contact with their child's foster carers need to understand how these arrangements will change.

Due to having a positive relationship with the birth parents, we were happy to send photos in letterbox contact. However, this was decided by others to only take place once per year. Unfortunately, we have not received any letters back as yet. The birth mother did try to contact us through social media but we have had to block her due to messages which clearly worried us in her understanding of adoption and the future. We are still left in the dark as to where we send future letterbox contact.
FCA 8

In some cases, the birth parents' awareness of the foster carers' identity may be a reason for deciding that ongoing contact is not appropriate, and anonymity as to the child's adopters may need to be preserved where risk factors have been identified. In these cases, the carer adopter's ability to display "communicative openness" – 'an open, honest, non-defensive, and emotionally attuned family dialogue, not only about adoption related issues' and to 'acknowledge and support the child's dual connection to two families, and perhaps to facilitate contact between these two family systems in one form or another' (Brodzinsky, 2006) will be particularly important.

It will be important to involve the agency's letterbox co-ordinator in setting up plans and ensuring that carer adopters know that the co-ordinator can offer help and guidance if their child's needs change as they get older. Birth family members also need to know who is available to help and support them with agreed letterbox or direct contact arrangements and to negotiate these changed relationships.

Carer adopters should also be made aware that where contact arrangements are not working after the adoption order has been made, they can seek support from the local authority. Further, if issues cannot be resolved through mediation, they can apply to court for an s.51A order where an agreement for some form of continuing contact had been made but was not adhered to, or for an s.51A(2)(b) order prohibiting contact where they have received unwanted, unsolicited and potentially harmful contact with the child.

> *I keep an extremely low social media profile and never post pictures of my son. However, there are plenty of pictures of me online and, although my son will look different over the years, I won't change that much.*
> FCA 1

SIBLING CONTACT

Contact with siblings is likely to have been in place whilst the child was being fostered and there may be existing relationships with those siblings and their carers. When planning future sibling contact post-order, rather than stick to accepted norms (for example, no direct contact with other siblings where there will be ongoing contact with birth parents), it is important to seek the views of the carer adopters about the contact arrangements that they could support, based both on the needs of the child but also taking into account their ability to manage issues that would perhaps not be so easy for adopters without those pre-existing relationships.

Adoption Statutory Guidance (DfE, 2013) – 7.11 states that:

> *Where siblings cannot be placed together with the same family, it is important to ensure that contact arrangements between them are given very careful attention and plans for maintaining contact are robust. Contact arrangements may need to be varied as the children's relationships and need for contact change over time.*

Several carer adopters commented to us about contact arrangements.

> *We felt the contact arrangements were suitable, sensitive and appropriate. We send a six-monthly letterbox letter to our daughter's birth mother and grandmother. The plan was for the children to have regular face-to-face contact with their siblings (who were adopted by their foster carers). However, their adoptive parents have said they are no longer willing to have ongoing contact, which is a huge loss for our daughters. It saddens me greatly that prospective adoptive parents are able to make promises and agreements re: ongoing contact and then rescind on these agreements once the adoption order is made. Our daughters were half of a very close sibling group of four and our eldest daughter played a protective, parenting role over her younger siblings. She currently has no idea where or how her brother and sister are and worries about them so much. I wish there was a way that post-adoption contact was legally binding (even if it had to be amended and adjusted*

to suit the changing needs of the children). This is a source of much sadness for our daughter.
FCA 6

They have not met her [birth mother] as direct contact had stopped before their son came to them. They have exchanged letters with her and she has said she wants him to be happy. They think she is waiting for a meeting when he is 18. They would support direct contact with her in the future if he wanted this. They have kept informal contact with his sisters who are also adopted in separate placements. They also support direct contact and the families meet up all together for birthdays and Christmas. They had an overseas holiday to see his sister and her family and use FaceTime to keep that contact going. They will spend holidays together with the other families. He phones three–four times a week with his older sister and with his younger sister, they speak several times a week and see her regularly. He says he wants to live next door to them all!
FCA 11 via social worker

KEY POINTS

- There should be a comprehensive adoption support plan in place and carer adopters should be given clear information about how to access support in the future, particularly when it is likely that support services may not be needed in the near future.

- Consideration should be given to early referral to the ASF where therapeutic services are identified to meet the child's needs during the matching process.

- Carer adopters should be routinely included and linked into adoption support services.

- Contact arrangements should be considered on an individual basis, taking account of the carer adopter's views and existing relationships.

Conclusion

We find it surprising and concerning that there has been no significant change in the number of children being adopted by their foster carers in the last 15 years, and that unlike in the USA, older children are still for the most part not being adopted in this way. Although there has been an increased focus on achieving adoption for children who cannot be cared for by their birth family, there has been little public debate or discussion about the potential contribution that existing foster carers could make to improving the chances of achieving adoption, particularly for those children who may be seen as "harder to place". However, there is now legislation in England, Wales and Northern Ireland which sets out the need to fast-track/give priority to these applications to avoid delay in care planning for the child, and this might serve as the catalyst needed to make progress in this area.

There is evidence from research that where agencies have clear policies for processing carer adoptions, this ensures that all staff have a shared understanding and give a consistent message to carers. Otherwise, both research and anecdotal evidence suggests that carer adopters have to negotiate a range of positive or negative views of individual social workers and managers in order to pursue their desire to legally parent a child they have come to care deeply about. It is also concerning that where adoption has been achieved in the context of conflict between carer adopters and the local authority, this has then impacted on the perceived availability or quality of adoption support.

Any agency policy needs to emphasise the benefits of foster carers adopting, and take account of their differing motivation from "stranger" adopters. This message should be widely disseminated to social workers, IROs and carers. In addition, whilst agency policies should be clear about expectations around financial support and whether carers should continue to foster, there should also be flexibility to take into account the circumstances of each individual case.

We would advocate that the potential for a foster carer wanting to adopt should be considered at an early stage in care planning for children so that carers can rule themselves in or out and have time to consider the implications for themselves and their families. The decision that adoption is the right plan for the child will be taken based on the circumstances of the child's history and where a return to their birth family has been ruled out. When their foster carer then expresses an interest in offering a permanent placement, social workers should explore the issues and routes to permanence with the carer in an open and transparent discussion, considering both the potential benefits but also any potential difficulties or reasons why it may not be in the child's best interests or meet their identified needs.

There should be joint working between fostering and adoption teams to enable full disclosure of all relevant information, and working across consortia or regional agencies to ensure specific preparation training can be provided for carers adopting, with an opportunity to meet others in a similar position. These informal networks may well be important for carer adopters after the adoption order has been made.

Finally, it is essential that carer adopters are given full information about their entitlement to adoption support for themselves and their child, not just at the time of the adoption but into the future. Comprehensive adoption support plans based on children's assessed needs will help with this but, given the many unknowns that come with children needing adoption, it is essential that carer adopters feel able to seek support in later years if this is needed.

The decision to adopt a child or children from foster care is life-changing, for both the child and their foster family. Evidence from other countries such as the USA and Northern Ireland would suggest that, with a more consistent and positive view of carer adoption, this opportunity could be extended to a wider number of children in care.

FINAL THOUGHTS FROM CARER ADOPTERS

Has it changed my relationship with my child? Well, yes and no. I already loved him, cared for him, put his needs first. Now I am able to add permanence and belonging to that. That doesn't change my love for him at all, but it will, I believe, give him the best chance for his future.
FCA 1

Adopting our daughter was the best thing we have ever done, she has brought so much joy to our lives.
FCA 2

Absolutely the best thing we did. She completed our family and made our world so much richer than it may have otherwise been. The boys have a sister, and we have a daughter, and I cannot imagine life without her.
FCA 3

I was already attached to her and wanted to provide her the best chance in life. For myself, I did not see myself having my own child and was very happy to create my family this way.
FCA 4

If I loved him any more I fear I would burst, as he is my world!
FCA 5

I'm not sure whether our eldest daughter feels a difference in terms of the quality of her relationship with us. I'd like to think that the way I parented her and cared for her as a foster carer was not dissimilar to how I parent her now (aside from being able to make decisions which I wouldn't have been able to do as a foster carer). However, the sense of permanence has definitely had a positive impact on all of us as well as just that feeling of being a "normal" family.
FCA 6

I can be a parent to him and not just a carer. I can offer him opportunities and access services to get him to be the best he can be within his ability range. I also wanted him to have a family so when I am not here he will always have family that love and care for him; he will never be alone.
FCA 7

Our simple advice to other foster carers thinking of adopting is to seek information and advice from anyone and everyone! Then follow your heart!
FCA 8

When asked if it was the right decision for her and her family to adopt, she (the foster carer) said, 'Definitely. He is loved and treated the same as our own birth children and they would have it no other way'.
FCA 10 via social worker

They would say, 'Go for it'. There may be problems, for them it came from his social worker but they would say think about the end goal, the security and your love for the child.
FCA 11 via social worker

It was the right decision for both of us and it has changed our relationship. R has been calmer, she has a lot to come to terms with and this will be difficult for her, I hope I can help her through this so she can reach her full potential.
FCA 12

We have been able to gain a good insight into R's history and supported him with contact. There has also been the opportunity for us all to develop a trusting bond and for R to think and decide about adoption and if he wanted to stay with us. This is something that we feel is positive for the child and for us as a family.
FCA 13

If you feel you have a strong attachment and bond with the child and feel it's the right thing to do for yourself, but most importantly for the child, then don't be scared to seek help and support in being able to offer a child a forever home.
FCA 14

Appendix 1
Case studies of foster carers who have adopted

FCA 1

FCA 1 lives with her adopted son and a foster child. FCA 1 had no children before she adopted. Her son was the first child she had fostered and he has lived with her for over three years since he was a very young baby.

Her son came into care at 18 weeks old, on an s.20 order. The care plan was for rehabilitation with his birth mother. He had previously lived with his birth mother at their maternal grandmother's house, and then at an emergency homeless shelter for a short period. The birth mother absconded from the shelter and refused to return, at which point her son came into care. He stayed with FCA 1 until shortly after his first birthday, at which point he returned to his birth mother who, by this time, had completed parenting classes and assessments and been rehomed at a parent and child home.

The rehabilitation lasted just over three weeks. The birth mother absconded again, leaving her son in the care of a teenager, and did not enquire as to his whereabouts for several days. He was placed with FCA 1 again, and the care plan was changed to adoption. Once family member assessments had been exhausted, FCA 1 asked to be considered to adopt him.

FCA 2

Seven people live at the home of FCA 2, including her husband and their three birth children, one fostered child and their adopted daughter. Their adopted daughter has lived with them since she was five days old. FCA 2 had initially fostered her and her birth mother, as a parent and child placement.

FCA 3

FCA 3 are a married couple, with two birth sons, aged 17 and 19. They had previously tried, unsuccessfully, to have another birth child after having their two sons. Their adopted child was placed with them as a fostering placement straight from hospital at two days old; she was adopted at three years old and is now aged nine. Her birth mother had mental health and learning difficulties, and her birth father was described as an "illegal immigrant".

They decided to apply to adopt her as she was 21 months old before the final care hearing concluded, and she had known no other home. They also knew that she would be classified as "hard to place" due to her mixed heritage and family history of mental health issues.

FCA 4

FCA 4 is a single carer who has two 21-year-olds who are living with her on a Staying Put arrangement, and a 14-year-old foster child. Her four-and-a-half-year-old adopted child has lived with her since birth. FCA 4 was asked to foster a 16-year-old, who was eight months pregnant, for four weeks pre-birth and six weeks after birth. They both remained with FCA 4 for six months, and then the birth mother decided to leave the placement without the baby. FCA 4 was present when the child was born and decided to adopt as she realised that the child would be over two years old when a decision about her future was made.

FCA 5

FCA 5 is a single carer and lives with her daughter, aged 24. Her daughter is in the process of purchasing her own property, and is therefore only at home temporarily. She also has an eight-year-old girl who lives with her as a long-term foster placement, and a two-year-old boy who she is in the process of adopting. He came to live with her straight from hospital. His birth family between them had had four previous children removed and one child had died. FCA 5 started considering adopting him when he was about 18 months old. He had a number of health problems and she felt he had an uncertain future.

FCA 6

FCA 6 and her husband have lived with their two adopted daughters for three-and-a-half years. They had a permanently fostered child living with them when the girls were first placed. He now lives independently, but is a regular visitor and very much part of the family. Their adopted daughters have two half-siblings who were placed with another foster carer who subsequently adopted them. The girls were placed with FCA 6 as a short-term foster placement with the intention that they would return home to their mother within a few months. As the assessment progressed, it was clear that the children could not return home and their care plan was changed to adoption. At this point, the couple applied to adopt them, having developed a strong attachment. Apart from their first night in emergency foster care, the children have lived only with this family since coming into care.

FCA 7

FCA 7 lives with her adult daughter, who is profoundly disabled, her 17-year-old daughter, who is visually impaired, and her adopted son. Although she had a 17-month-old in a fostering placement already, she initially agreed to look after him as she had a good knowledge of the care of pre-term babies. She collected him from hospital when he was six weeks old. He was relinquished, has met his mother and has had a goodbye visit. He has evolving disabilities and is of dual heritage. FCA 7 was aware he would be difficult to find a family for and was asked if she would offer long-term fostering, but decided she would prefer to adopt him.

FCA 8

FCA 8 lives with her husband, their two birth sons (aged 11 and eight) and their adopted son, who is aged two-and-a-half. The couple fostered him from within hours of his birth. His birth parents had failed a pre-birth assessment and further assessments whilst he was in care. As foster carers, they were matched to him as a newborn baby, as this was where their experience had excelled. When he was nine months old they decided to apply to adopt him.

FCA 9

FCA 9 lives with her husband, birth son (24 years old), their two adopted daughters (19 and 7 years old), and their adopted son (nine years old). They are also fostering babies. All three adopted children were fostered from birth. The oldest child's mother was an alcoholic; the nine-year-old's mother was addicted to heroin; and the seven-year-old's mother had special needs.

FCA 10

FCA 10's adopted son was placed with her straight from hospital at two-and-a-half weeks old. He was in the special care unit after his birth. His mother was a substance abuser and he was born with a visual impairment, cerebral palsy and developmental delay.

All the family came to love him and thought of him as their own child. They felt they could give him the care he needed and a good quality of life and so they decided to adopt him. They have continued to foster but decided to care for older children as they also had their own baby son, so the two children were very close in age.

FCA 11

FCA 11 are a couple who live with their 14-year-old adopted son. The male carer also has two adult birth children. Their adopted son was placed after experiencing a number of previous foster placements and the breakdown of a long-term placement. They took him expecting that it could become a long-term arrangement. They had thought about offering long-term fostering, maybe leading to adoption. His three sisters had all been adopted and he then asked them to adopt him.

FCA 12

FCA 12 lives with her adult son and foster daughter, aged six. She is currently adopting her foster daughter, who was placed with her just over a year ago, aged five. This has been her daughter's only foster placement but she had lived in a number of homes before coming into care.

The original care plan was for long-term fostering or adoption and FCA 12 decided to offer a long-term placement, but further assessment led to a view that adoption would be the preferred option.

FCA 13

FCA 13 are a white couple in their early 50s. They are experienced parents, have adopted a boy and fostered several children. They are fostering an eight-year-old dual heritage boy who was placed with them and then returned to his birth mother. This did not work and he returned to their care. The child was adamant that he wished to remain with his foster family and be adopted by them. They were in complete agreement with his wishes. The adoption order application has been lodged.

FCA 14

FCA 14 are a white couple in their late 40s who have several birth children and have fostered for many years. They adopted one foster child several years ago, having cared for him since he was several weeks old; he is now a teenager. They are now adopting a second young boy, who has some complex health and developmental needs. He was previously linked to another adoptive family who pulled out at the introductions stage. The birth family is aware of this plan and is supportive.

Appendix 2
Examples of agency process and policy documents

Leeds City Council: Foster carer adoption process flowchart

Foster carers can express an interest in applying to adopt the child/ren they are currently caring for by contacting the adoption advice line, or via the social worker

Adoption Duty completes the initial enquiry form (FCA) and forwards it to ATA, or the foster carer completes this and sends it to ATA

ATA to put information on fwi and forwards to ATM (via email) for allocation. ATM to inform AAO who the visit has been allocated to so that fwi can be updated. Adoption adviser to be allocated at this time to assist with the process

Prior to arranging an IHV, the allocated worker will:

- Contact the child's social worker to discuss the case and ascertain their views about the application

- Contact the SSW to ascertain their views about the application and thoughts about future fostering. This should if possible be confirmed in writing, shared with the foster carer at the IHV and included in the IHV report

- If the foster carers are approved by Leeds, establish when their last DBS checks were undertaken

- IHV letter 1 (FCA) to be sent out, with the advice about DBS checks if needed

AT the IHV, it is important to discuss:

- The foster carer's expectations about the financial support required and the department's position made clear

- The foster carer's views about future fostering

- Where possible, the child's social worker and SSW should attend the IHV

After the IHV:

- The ASW will write up the IHV on fwi, make a clear recommendation and pass it to the ATM

- If appropriate, book the applicants on an appropriate training course, either through the department or consortium

Where additional financial support is required, a submission should be made to the financial panel, at this point, by the social worker, prior to the matter being progressed further. Once this has been agreed, FCA Letter 2 will be sent by the ATM, confirming the financial support involved. The foster carers will be asked to sign and return an agreement accepting this proposal

The allocated ASW will be responsible for chasing this up with the foster carers and if there is any delay or disagreement, for arranging a meeting in the office where this can be discussed

Acceptance of finance form to be returned to AAO and put on fwi

Registration of Interest form to be sent out (FCA Letter 3). When returned, all other necessary checks to be completed by ATA

DBS need completing if this has not been renewed in the last 12 months

FCA Letter 4 to be sent out and amended as necessary. This advises the foster carers on how to submit DBS information/send medical form/SSAFA checks, etc

Medicals: it is important to establish when the last medical was undertaken. Normally, new medicals should be requested; however, if they have been undertaken recently by fostering, this may not be required and a decision could be made not to do so. However, the medicals should be sent to the medical adviser again for additional comments in relation to adoption. ATA are able to process this

fwi process: when the Stage 1 process is entered in fwi, AAO/ATM to submit early outcome option – this allows Stage 1/Stage 2 process to be open simultaneously. However, the Stage 1 process is to be completed on return of all appropriate checks

Approved foster carers may be able to move straight to Stage 2 and receive a tailored assessment, taking account of their circumstances. It is expected that foster carer adoption assessments will be completed in four months in total, where possible

The completed assessment (and match) will be considered by the adoption panel in the usual way

It is important that the fostering service provides a report for the adoption panel, detailing the carer's current and future fostering status, and their view of the proposed adoption

Once the panel has recommended the adoption approval and match, and this has been approved by the agency decision-maker, a formal planning meeting must be held. The meeting should include the foster carer/adopter, ASW, SSW, and the ASW who has completed the assessment. An adoption placement plan should be drawn up in the usual way and all necessary notifications will need to be sent

Post-approval finance issues: IFP foster carer

- When undertaking an adoption assessment with foster carers approved by an IFP, at the point of submitting paperwork to the adoption panel, the applicants will need to complete their bank details on the BACS payment form. This will reduce the time it takes to set up their payment if the match is approved

- Send both the BACS form and a copy of the letter confirming the financial arrangements to the Placement Service Payments Team prior to the panel

- Post-panel, confirm the agency decision with the Payments Team so they can commence payments as needed

Post-approval finance issues: Leeds foster carer

- Post-panel, confirm the agency decision with the Payments Team and send a copy of the letter confirming the financial arrangements

Key

fwi: Framework I (electronic system)

IHV: Initial Home Visit

AAO: Adoption Admin Officer

ATA: Adoption Team Admin

ATM: Adoption Team Manager

ADA: Adoption Adviser

ASW: Adoption Social Worker

SSW: Supervising Social Worker

Created by Margaret Orchard, February 2015
Reproduced with permission from Leeds City Council

Essex Adoption Service: Fast-track process for the assessment of second-time adopters, foster carers and connected carers

Assessment process: approved foster carers, connected carers or adopters where there is a child identified

Where a foster carer or connected carer who has been approved under the Fostering Regulations 2011 applies to adopt a child in their care, they should be reminded that they will still be subject to a full assessment as suitable to adopt (where they have not previously been dually approved for fostering and adoption). It must also be assessed whether an adoptive placement for this child with this particular carer is the most appropriate placement.

The key people involved in the case, e.g. CiCSW, CASW, relevant team managers, senior practitioner and any supervising social worker involved with the child and the carer, will discuss the viability (particularly if an adopter who was previously approved for a named child is being considered for a subsequent sibling).

Where there is potentially viability, a pre-assessment visit will be undertaken by the adoption social worker within 10 working days.

Where the application is thought not to be viable and therefore unlikely to progress, the team manager will give feedback to the adopter and explain in writing why the application will not progress at this time.

The outcome of this visit will be recorded within 10 working days and a professionals' meeting will be convened, chaired by the adoption team manager, to determine the viability as a result of the visit. This meeting will act as a Family Linking Meeting (FLM) and the Matching Matrix will be used. The purpose of the FLM is to evidence the carer's capacity to meet the child's identified needs and to highlight actions/outstanding issues to keep on target. The matching needs should be known from ADM Plan stage and the matrix should be added to throughout the process.

Where the assessment is to continue, the RTT issues the Registration of Interest (ROI) form to the applicant which must be returned immediately. Once received by the RTT, this starts the assessment process (Stages 1 and 2). Any checks will be undertaken by RTT simultaneously where they are required, bearing in mind that as foster carers, some of the information will have already been gathered during the course of their fostering role and may still be in date. The RTT will need to move the pathway to the end of Stage 1 to allow Stage 2 to be opened. Once the appropriate references and checks have been received, Stage 1 should be signed off on Protocol (ideally within two months).

The Stage 2 process may be followed as soon as the ROI has been received and a social worker allocated, bearing in mind that the relevant checks, references and medical must be received by the agency in order for the case to be considered by panel.

Where the fast track is to be followed, the applicant will be encouraged to complete the workbook and will have access to the preparation training (although for second-time adopters this will not always be a requirement, unless their previous approval and placement was prior to the introduction of the two-stage process).

Approved adopter/foster carer/connected carer expresses an interest in adopting a particular child

Case workers involved in case (CiCSW/CASW/SSW/TMs) discuss viability

Decision to Proceed

No → Applicant notified by adoption team manager who will give feedback and close the enquiry

Yes → Pre-assessment visit undertaken by adoption social worker within 10 days. Social worker informs the RTT team via email, giving the date of the visit

Professionals' Meeting, acting as a Family Linking Meeting, within 10 days of an initial visit, chaired by Locality Adoption Manager. Fostering to bring Form F to the meeting. Adoption to bring previous PAR

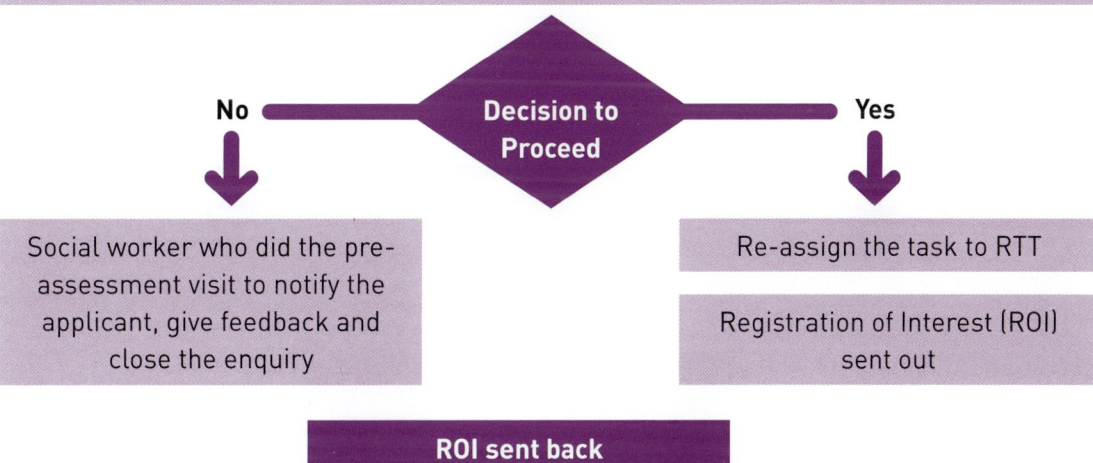

Decision to Proceed

No → Social worker who did the pre-assessment visit to notify the applicant, give feedback and close the enquiry

Yes → Re-assign the task to RTT

Registration of Interest (ROI) sent out

ROI sent back

Within five days, RTT confirm receipt of ROI and checks/reference process launch

Stage 2 pathway opened and followed by locality team

When all required references received, RTT close Stage 1 on Protocol

Note: RTT will liaise with Fostering for information on checks which will only be done if required. Applicants will be encouraged to complete the workbook and the preparation training

Key
CICSW: Child's Allocated Social Worker
CASW: Child's Adoption Social Worker
RTT: Adoption Recruitment and Training Team
FLM: Family Linking Meeting

Reproduced with permision from Essex County Council

Appendix 3
Adapted CoramBAAF forms which can be used for carer adoptions

Registration of Interest form for foster carers wishing to adopt a child in their care

Name of Applicant 1

Name of Applicant 2

I confirm that I would like to register my interest in being assessed to adopt *name of child/ren* **with**

Name of adoption agency

Date

Signature of Applicant 1

Signature of Applicant 2

The following information enables your adoption agency to work with you during the adopter assessment process and to undertake the required statutory checks. Some additional forms will need to be completed once your registration has been accepted to enable police and medical checks to be obtained. If you have any queries or concerns about providing the information requested here, contact the Adoption Team to discuss this.

	Applicant 1	**Applicant 2**
Surname		
First name/s		
Other names used (including former or familiar names)		
Date of birth and age		
Place of birth		

Telephone – daytime

Telephone – evening

Mobile no.

Email

Preferred method of contact

Address

Home address

Postcode

How long have you lived at this address?

Is this your permanent place of residence? If not, please give details   Yes/No   Yes/No

Name of the local authority area in which you live

If you have lived in your current address for less than 10 years, please give your previous addresses for each applicant below:

Address	From	To

Partnership status

	Applicant 1	Applicant 2
If you are married, or have a registered civil partnership, give date and place of marriage/registration		
If you are living with a partner, date on which you set up a household together		
If you are separated, divorced, have dissolved a civil partnership or ended a relationship where you had set up a household together, give the date and the name of your previous partner/s		
Have you ever parented children with previous partners? If so, please give details		

Identity

	Applicant 1	Applicant 2
Sex		
Nationality		
Ethnicity		
Primary language spoken in the home		
Other language(s) spoken in the home		
Do you need any support during the assessment with language spoken, i.e. an interpreter? If yes, give details.	Yes/No	Yes/No
Religion or faith group		
Are you practising or non-practising?		
Do you consider yourself as having a disability? If yes, give details.	Yes/No	Yes/No

Who else lives in the household? (Include the child/ren you wish to adopt and any other foster children)

Children under 18

Surname	First name/s	Sex M/F	Date of birth	Ethnicity	Relationship to applicant(s)	Current school

Adults (including grown-up children) living in your household

Surname	First name/s	Sex M/F	Date of birth	Ethnicity	Relationship to applicant(s)	Are they in education/ employment/retired?

Are there other adults (not living in your household) who may have responsibility on a regular basis for the care of any child/ren placed with you?

Surname	First name/s	Sex M/F	Date of birth	Ethnicity	Relationship to applicant(s)

Do you have any children (under 18) from a current or previous partnership living elsewhere?

Surname	First name/s	Sex M/F	Date of birth	Ethnicity	Relationship to applicant(s)

Do you have any adult children living elsewhere?

Surname	First name/s	Sex M/F	Date of birth	Ethnicity	Relationship to applicant(s)

Fostering Service Provider (FSP) details

Give name and address of FSP and fostering manager	
Date you started fostering for your current FSP	

Occupation

	Applicant 1	Applicant 2
Job title (if employed)		
Current employer and address (if any)		
Date started		
Current hours of work		
Income from occupation or profession		
Proposed hours of work following placement of child for adoption		

Have you previously worked with children or vulnerable adults? If so, please list the employers' names and addresses below.

Residence

Is your main home currently in the UK?	
If not, state where your main home is	
How long have you been living in the UK?	
If you are a non-UK passport holder, state country of issue	

If you are a non-UK passport holder or European Economic Area (EEA) citizen, do you have permanent residency in the UK?

If not, how long have you lived in the UK?

If you are a non-UK and non-EEA citizen, do you have indefinite leave to remain in the UK?

Checks

Have you ever had a county court judgement made against you or have you ever been declared bankrupt?　　　Yes/No

If yes, please give date(s), court and brief details.

Have you been involved in any family court proceedings or in any proceedings about a child/children and/or family?　　　Yes/No

If yes, give details of the date, name of court, type of order made and the name of the child/children concerned.

Have you previously applied to become a foster carer, adopter or childminder?　　　Yes/No

If yes, give details of the date, name of the agency, address, and outcome.

Has any other member of your household previously applied to become a foster carer, adopter or childminder?　　　Yes/No

If yes, give details of the date, name of agency, address, and outcome.

Have you ever lived or worked abroad since you were aged 18, or have you ever served in the armed forces? If so, please give details

Health

	Applicant 1	**Applicant 2**
Name of your GP		
Address of your GP practice		
Telephone		
How long have you been registered with your GP?		

Referees

Please give the names and addresses of three people who know you both well and over a period of time and who would be prepared to be interviewed about your parenting/caring capacity and other issues relevant to this application. Only one of these referees should be a family member.

NB Please note these are minimum requirements and the agency may require additional references where applicable.

	Referee	Referee	Referee
Name			
Address			
Relationship to you			
Number of years known			
Does this referee know you as a couple (if joint application) or just one of you?			

Declaration

I certify that, to the best of my knowledge and belief, the details supplied in this registration of interest are correct. I understand that the agency may seek verification of any of the facts supplied. I understand that if any of this information is found to be false or misleading, this may result in the agency deciding not to proceed to an assessment of my application to adopt.

I confirm that I have not currently registered my interest with any other adoption agency.

I understand that the agency may ask me to supply further information in order to make the decision to proceed to an assessment of my application.

I understand that any information supplied by me in respect of my application to adopt may be held and/or processed in an electronic form and is subject to the relevant provisions in the Data Protection Act 1998 and other relevant statutes. I understand that any information supplied will form part of the agency's case record held in respect of my application.

I understand that the agency will contact me within five working days of receiving my registration of interest. My availability to be contacted during this period is as follows: [applicant to complete]

Consents

I give my consent to the agency asking for information (written or verbal) from the individuals, agencies or organisations identified by me or by the agency in support of this registration of interest. I understand that any information obtained will only be used in processing my application to adopt.

I give my consent to the agency requesting a police check from the Disclosure and Barring Service. I understand that the appropriate forms will be given to me once my registration has been accepted.

I consent to the agency requesting a written report from my GP about my health once my registration has been accepted and I agree to arranging and taking part in a medical examination by my registered medical practitioner who will then provide a written report, and to any further enquiry deemed necessary. (I understand that further enquiries from medical specialists may be needed, and that in future I may be asked to give specific consent to obtain further health information.)

Signature _____ Date _____

Print name _____

Signature _____ Date _____

Print name _____

Agency details (to be completed by agency)

Agency reference number _____

Name of agency _____

Address _____

Postcode _____

Telephone _____

Name of team manager _____

Telephone _____

Minicom _____

Fax _____

Email _____

Assessment Agreement (Plan) for a Reg 30F Assessment (foster carer adopting)

This is an agreement between _____ (Name of applicant/s) and

_____ (Name of adoption agency)

This agreement sets out how we will work with you on a "fast track" assessment (Adoption Agency Regulations 30F 3 (AAR), now that you have applied to adopt a child who is already placed with you as a foster child. We want to make sure that you are able to explore what adoption will mean for you and your family at a pace that is right for you. This agreement will help us to work with you and give you information about the work that we will be doing and the things we will ask you to do. We will be completing the necessary checks on you at the same time as working on your assessment so we aim to meet the four month timescale set out in the AAR. This agreement can be reviewed at the request of either party.

Checks

We will undertake checks with the Disclosure and Barring Service (DBS) and local authorities where you have lived; we will contact your personal references and request access to your fostering records held by your fostering service provider; and we will obtain a view from the agency medical adviser on your completed medicals. We may also ask you for information to take up additional checks where needed, e.g. to contact significant previous partners or any adult children or other professionals, e.g. schools involved with your foster child.

We will ask you to provide us with all the information we need to undertake these checks, including attending your GP for a medical examination at an early stage to try and avoid delays in obtaining the information required by our agency medical adviser to give their view. We will keep you informed of any delays we experience in obtaining the information we need to complete the required checks.

Preparation/training

You will already have completed some relevant training as a foster carer. We have identified the following preparation/training/self-evaluation work/reading for you to complete to understand more about your role as an adoptive parent. All the relevant materials which will be provided for you or signposted to by the agency and dates of proposed training are set out below.

We think it is important that you complete all the identified preparation and training at a pace which feels right for you. If you decide you wish to take longer than the four months set out for your assessment, this can be discussed and agreed with your social worker.

Details of the assessment

It is proposed that there will be *(insert number)* of assessment sessions over the next three months. This will be the minimum requirement needed to complete the assessment. We will discuss with you any need for additional sessions that is identified during the assessment or undertaken as standard within this agency.

There will also be additional meetings or contact arranged with (name(s) of child/ren at home or living away from home *(insert where appropriate)*

Each session will last between one and two-and-a-half hours and will be held at your home or at the agency's office as agreed below.

The assessment will start on *(date of first assessment visit)*.

Date of visit	Time and venue of visit/meeting	Who will be involved	What areas will be covered

It is anticipated that the date of completion of the assessment report will be [*date*].

A second opinion visit may be undertaken if needed by another social worker or team manager following completion of the report.

We anticipate that the report will be ready to be presented to the adoption panel on [*give date and venue*].

We will discuss with you whether we need to make contingency plans where a worker is going on extended annual leave or goes off sick for an extended period, and will discuss and agree a solution with you.

We will all agree to prioritise meetings and come prepared with agreed tasks promptly completed. If either party cannot make a planned visit, they will let people know in good time so that a new date can be arranged. If you have had to cancel visits or decide you would like to take some time out from the assessment, this may require the panel date to be delayed.

We would expect that this assessment will be completed within four months. Where there are delays on behalf of the agency, we will let you know and give you reasons verbally and in writing and take all reasonable steps to minimise the length of these delays.

It is important that you feel you can decide that you want to take a break or slow down the process at any time if you wish to do so. Initially, we would ask you to discuss this with your assessing social worker, following this up with putting your reasons in writing for our case files.

Working in partnership

It is important during the adoption process that there is a commitment to an honest and open exchange between you and the social workers you will meet. This is an essential part of our working relationship with you. We would ask that you share full information with us and do not withhold any information about things that may influence your capacity to care for a child. If you are unsure about the impact of sharing any information, please discuss this with us.

We will discuss any issues or concerns that may emerge from the checks with you so there is an opportunity to resolve them wherever possible. If there is information that is provided from references or statutory checks, we will share as full information as possible but any third party information will have to take account of data protection principles.

If we decide we cannot proceed with the assessment as a result of information from the references or statutory checks, we will provide you with a written explanation of the reasons and give you information about our complaints process.

We will discuss any issues or concerns that may emerge from the assessment with you so there is an opportunity to resolve them wherever possible. If we are not recommending your approval at the end of the assessment process, you will be given information about the process for submitting representations or applying to the Independent Review Mechanism (IRM).

You will be given contact details for the adoption team manager so you can get in touch with them at any time if you have concerns about the progress of your assessment or want to request a review of the assessment agreement.

Any other points to be covered

```
```

Signatures

Signature of Applicant 1   Date

Print name

Signature of Applicant 2   Date

Print name

Signature of social worker

Signature   Date

Print name

Signature of team manager on behalf of the agency

Signature   Date

Print name

CoramBAAF guide to completion of Annex A Report referencing the relevant sections of CPR/PAR/APR reports

Requirements of Annex A Report to the court where there has been an application for an adoption order or an application for a Section 84 order	Information set out in CPR/Annex B Report (CPR should have been updated for the match but may need some further updating)
Section A: The report and matters for the proceedings	**Section A: The report and matters for the proceedings**
Part 1: The report For each of the principal author/s of the report: i: Name ii: Role in relation to this case iii: Sections completed in this report iv: Qualifications and experience v: Name and address of the adoption agency and vi: Adoption agency case reference number	**Part 1: The report** For each of the principal authors of the report: i: Name ii: Role in relation to this case iii: Sections completed in this report iv: Qualifications and experience v: Name and address of the adoption agency and vi: Adoption agency case reference number
Part 2: Matters for the proceedings (a) Whether the adoption agency considers that any other person should be made a respondent or a party to the proceedings, including the child. (b) Whether any of the respondents is under the age of 18. (c) Whether a respondent is a person who, by reason of mental disorder within the meaning of the Mental Health Act 1983, is incapable of managing and administering his or her property and affairs. If so, medical evidence should be provided with particular regard to the effect on that person's ability to make decisions in the proceedings.	**Part 2: Matters for the proceedings** (a) Whether the adoption agency considers that any other person should be made a respondent or a party to the proceedings. (b) Whether any of the respondents is under the age of 18. (c) Whether a respondent is a person who, by reason of mental disorder within the meaning of the Mental Health Act 1983, is incapable of managing and administering his or her property and affairs. If so, medical evidence should be provided with particular regard to the effect on that person's ability to make decisions in the proceedings.

Section B: The child and the birth family

Part 1	Part 1
Information about the child	**Information about the child**
(a) Name, sex, date and place of birth and address, including local authority area.	* Essential information on the child
(b) Photograph and physical description.	Front sheet and 9.1: Physical description
(c) Nationality.	3: Essential information on the child
(d) Racial origin and cultural and linguistic background.	5: Family composition 9.6–9.8: Description of the child – identity, language 9.7: Description of the child – religion
(e) Religious persuasion (including details of baptism, confirmation or equivalent ceremonies).	
(f) Details of any siblings, half-siblings and step-siblings, including dates of birth.	5: Family composition – may need updating
(g) Whether the child is looked after by a local authority.	6: Legal status of the child – update with PO
(h) Whether the child has been placed for adoption with the prospective adopter by a UK adoption agency.	Not covered
(i) Whether the child was being fostered by the prospective adopter.	If yes, would be covered in PAR
(j) Whether the child was brought into the UK for adoption, including date of entry and whether an adoption order was made in the child's country of origin.	Not covered
(k) Personality and social development, including emotional and behavioural management and any related needs.	9.2, 9.4, 9.5: Description of the child – personality, self-care skills, emotional, behavioural and social development – updated
(l) Details of interests, likes and dislikes.	9.3: Description of the child – interests, likes and dislikes – updated

* The numbers in this section refer to the numbering in the CPR form

(m) A summary, written by the agency's medical adviser, of the child's health history, his current state of health and any need for health care that is anticipated, and the date of the most recent medical examination.	9.9: Child's health; 10: Summary report from medical adviser + LAC medical most recent, updated if required
(n) Any known learning difficulties or known general medical or mental health factors that are likely to have, or may have, genetic implications.	11: The child's education; 10: Child's health
(o) Names, addresses and types of nurseries or schools attended, with dates.	11: The child's education
(p) Educational attainments.	11: The child's education
(q) Any special needs in relation to the child (whether physical, learning, behavioural or any other) and his emotional and behavioural development.	11: The child's education
(r) Whether the child is subject to a statement under the Education Act 1996.	11: The child's education
(s) Previous orders concerning the child: i: the name of the court; ii: the order made; and iii: the date of the order.	6: Legal status of the child – update with details of CO and PO 6: Legal status of the child
(t) Inheritance rights and any claim to damages under the Fatal Accidents Act 1976 the child stands to retain or lose if adopted.	
(u) Any other relevant information which might assist the court.	14.2: Any other relevant information
ii: Information about each parent of the child	**Part 1: Information about child's parents and other significant people**
(a) Name, date and place of birth and address (date on which last address was confirmed current), including local authority area.	15: The child's birth mother; 20: the child's birth father – ensure last address is provided and data obtained
(b) Photograph, if available, and physical description.	15.1 & 20.1: Photo and description

(c) Nationality.	
(d) Racial origin and cultural and linguistic background.	15: The child's birth mother; 20: The child's birth father
(e) Whether the mother and father were married to each other at the time of the child's birth, or have subsequently married.	21: Relationship between the birth mother and birth father
(f) Where the parent has been previously married or entered into a civil partnership, dates of those marriages or civil partnerships.	17/22: Summary and brief social history of birth mother/Summary and brief social history of birth father
(g) Where the mother and father are not married, whether the father has parental responsibility and, if so, how it was acquired.	18: Birth father with PR for the child; 19: Birth father without PR – update if PR granted during proceedings
(h) If the identity or whereabouts of the father are not known, the information about him that has been ascertained and from whom, and the steps that have been taken to establish paternity.	19: Birth father without PR
(i) Past and present relationship with the other parent	
(j) Other information about the parent, where available:	21: Relationship between the birth mother and birth father – update as needed
	17/15.6: Summary and brief social history of birth mother/home and neighbourhood in which she lives
	22/20/6: Summary and brief social history of birth father/home and neighbourhood in which he lives
i: Health, including any known learning difficulties or known general medical or mental health factors which are likely to have, or may have, genetic implications;	15.7/20.7: Brief summary of any health factors – birth mother/Brief summary of any health factors – birth father
ii: religious persuasion;	5: Family composition
iii: educational history;	15.3/20.3: Educational history – birth mother/Educational history – birth father
iv: employment history; and	15.4/15.5/20.4/20.5: Current occupation and employment history – birth mother/ Current occupation and employment history – birth father

v: personality and interests.	15.2: Personality and interests of birth mother; 20.2: Personality and interests of birth father 14.2: Any other relevant information
(k) Any other relevant information which might assist the court.	
Part 2: Relationships, contact arrangements and views	**Part 2: Contact arrangements**
The child (a) If the child is in the care of a local authority or voluntary organisation, or has been, details (including dates) of any placements with foster carers, or other arrangements in respect of the care of the child, including particulars of the persons with whom the child has had his home and observations on the care provided.	8. Chronology of the child's care since birth; 12.2: Summary of child's history – update with details of adoptive placement
(b) The child's wishes and feelings (if appropriate, having regard to the child's age and understanding) about the application, its consequences, and adoption, including any wishes in respect of religious and cultural upbringing. (c) The child's wishes and feelings in relation to contact (if appropriate, having regard to the child's age and understanding). (d) The child's wishes and feelings recorded in any other proceedings. (e) Date when the child's views were last ascertained.	14: Child's wishes and feelings; 14.1: Social worker's analysis of the wishes and feelings of the child – would need to be updated to include views since adoptive placement
The child's parents (or guardian) and relatives (a) The parents' wishes and feelings about the application, its consequences, and adoption, including any wishes in respect of the child's religious and cultural upbringing.	

(b) Each parent's (or guardian's) wishes and feelings in relation to contact. (c) Date/s when the views of each parent or guardian were last ascertained.	30: Support to birth mother; 31: Support to birth father – will need update since adoptive placement
(d) Arrangements concerning any siblings, including half-siblings and step-siblings, and whether any are the subject of a parallel application or have been the subject of any orders. If so, for each case give: i) the name of the court; ii) the order made, or (if proceedings are pending) the order applied for; and iii) the date of order, or date of next hearing if proceedings are pending.	24: Child's siblings with any updated needed Part 2: Contact arrangements
(f) The relationship which the child has with relatives, and with any other person considered relevant, including:	25: Other significant relatives or relevant people
i: the likelihood of any such relationship continuing and the value to the child of its doing so; and ii: the ability and willingness of any of the child's relatives, or of any such person, to provide the child with a secure environment in which the child can develop, and otherwise to meet the child's needs.	26: Current contact arrangements for the child; 27: Planned contact arrangements and details after placement and after adoption and any update
(g) The wishes and feelings of any of the child's relatives, or of any such person, regarding the child.	25: Other significant relatives or relevant people – update as needed
(h) Dates when the views of members of the child's wider family and any other relevant person were last ascertained.	
Part 3: Summary of the actions of the adoption agency	**Part 3: Summary of the actions of the adoption agency**
(a) Brief account of the agency's actions in the case, with particulars and dates of all written information and notices given to the child and his parents and any person with PR.	29: Chronology of the decisions and actions taken by the agency with respect to the child; update from point of matching

(b) If consent has been given for the child to be placed for adoption, and also consent for the child to be adopted, the names of those who gave consent and the date such consents were given. If such consents were subsequently withdrawn, the dates of these withdrawals.	6: Legal status of the child – only need update if parent/s decide to withdraw consent
(c) If any statement has been made under section 20(4)(a) of the 2002 Act that a parent or guardian does not wish to be informed of any application for an adoption order, the names of those who have made such statements and the dates the statements were made. If such statements were subsequently withdrawn, the dates of these withdrawals.	6: Legal status of the child – only update if parent/s decide to withdraw consent
(d) Whether an order has been made under section 21 of the 2002 Act, section 18 of the Adoption (Scotland) Act 1978 or Article 17(1) or 18(1) of the Northern Ireland Order 1987.	Legal status – add date of PO
(e) Details of the support and advice given to the parents and any services offered or taken up.	30: Support to birth mother; 31: Support to birth father – update as needed
(f) If the father does not have parental responsibility, details of the steps taken to inform him of the application for an adoption order.	Not covered as requires current actions
(g) Brief details and dates of assessments of the child's needs, including expert opinions.	33: Brief details of assessments of the child's needs, giving date undertaken and expert's opinion
(h) Reasons for considering that adoption would be in the child's best interests (with date of relevant decision and reasons for any delay in implementing the decision)	34: Summary of the reason for considering that adoption would be in the child's best interests (with date of relevant decision and reasons for any delay in implementing the decision but with updating relevant to the adoption placement). New balance sheet needed re any update to birth parents/other relevant family members and covering welfare of the child.

	Information set out in PAR or APR
Section C: The prospective adopter of the child	**Section C: The prospective adopter of the child**
Part 1: Information about the prospective adopter, including suitability to adopt	
(a) Name, date and place of birth and address (date on which last address was confirmed current) including local authority area	Front sheet, Part 2 Factual information
(b) Photograph and physical description.	Front sheet – physical description may be in pen picture
(c) Whether the prospective adopter is domiciled or habitually resident in a part of the British Islands and, if habitually resident, for how long they have been resident.	Part 2 Factual information – verification and required checks
(d) Racial origin and cultural and linguistic background.	Part 2 Factual information – identity
(e) Marital status or civil partnership status, date and place of most recent marriage (if any) or civil partnership (if any).	Part 2 Factual information – partnership status
(f) Details of any previous marriage, civil partnership, or relationship where the prospective adopter lived with another person as a partner in an enduring family relationship.	Part 2 Factual information – partnership status
(g) Relationship (if any) to the child.	Confirm if either family member or previous foster carer
(h) Where adopters wish to adopt as a couple, the status of the relationship and an assessment of the stability and permanence of their relationship.	Part 1 Assessment report (6 relationships and support networks), update if any change
(i) If a married person or a civil partner is applying alone, the reasons for this.	Part 1 Assessment report (6 Relationships and support networks), update if any change

(j) Description of how the prospective adopter relates to adults and children.	Part 1 Assessment report (6 relationships and support networks; 14–16: Understanding of the needs of adopted children and adoptive parenting capacity) –
(k) Previous experience of caring for children (including as a step-parent, foster carer, child-minder or prospective adopter) and assessment of ability in this respect, together where appropriate with assessment of ability in bringing up the prospective adopter's own children.	Part 1 Assessment report (1 Family background and early experience; 6-7 Relationships and support networks) Part 2 Factual information – who else lives in the household
(l) A summary, written by the agency's medical adviser, of the prospective adopter's health history, current state of health and any need for health care which is anticipated, and date of most recent medical examination.	Part 1 Assessment report (4 Adult life – work, health and other issues) Part 2 Factual information – verification and checks required and medical adviser summary of the health and support needs of the applicant – provide any update from point of match
(m) Assessment of ability and sustainability to bring up the child throughout his childhood.	May be covered in APR – but to be updated with reference to this child
(n) Details of income and comments on the living standards of the household with particulars of the home and living conditions (and particulars of any home where the prospective adopter proposes to live with the child, if different).	Part 2 Factual information – the home and its environment – update as necessary, especially re income
(o) Details of other members of the household, including any children of the prospective adopter even if not resident in the household.	Part 2 Factual information – who else lives in the household – update from placement
(p) Details of the parents and any siblings of the prospective adopter, with their ages or ages at death	Part 1: Assessment report; family tree section 1
(q) Other information about the prospective adopter:	Part 2 Factual information – identity Part 1 Assessment report (2: Summary of education experiences)

i: religious persuasion; ii: educational history; iii: employment history; and iv: personality and interests	Part 1: Assessment report (3: Summary of employment) – may need update from point of placement Part 1 Assessment report (6: Relationships and support networks)
(r) Confirmation that the applicants have not been convicted of, or cautioned for, a specified offence within the meaning of regulation 23(3) of the Adoption Agencies Regulations 2005 (S.I. 2005/389)	Part 2 Factual information – statutory and other
(s) Confirmation that the prospective adopter is still approved.	
(t) Confirmation that any referee has been interviewed, with a report of their views and opinion of the weight to be placed thereon and whether they are still valid.	Part 2 Summary of personal references completed – updated from point of placement
(u) Details of any previous family court proceedings in which the prospective adopter has been involved (which have not been referred to elsewhere in this report).	Part 2 Factual information – checks, statutory and other
Part 2: Wishes, views and contact arrangements **Prospective adopter**	
(a) Whether the prospective adopter is willing to follow any wishes of the child or his parents or guardian in respect of the child's religious and cultural upbringing.	Should be included in the APR
(b) The views of other members of the prospective adopter's household and wider family in relation to the proposed adoption.	Part 1 Assessment report (6-8: Relationships and support networks) – updating
(c) Reasons for the prospective adopter wishing to adopt the child and extent of understanding of the nature and effect of adoption. Whether the prospective adopter has discussed adoption with the child.	Part 1 Assessment report (12-16: Becoming adopters – the assessment of adoptive parenting capacity) – needs to be updated relevant to this child since placement
(d) Any hope and expectations the prospective adopter has for the child's future.	Update from APR
(e) The prospective adopter's wishes and feelings in relation to contact.	Update from APR

Part 3: Actions of the adoption agency	
(a) Brief account of the agency's actions in the case, with particulars and dates of all written information and notices given to the prospective adopter.	**Set out from point of match and placement**
(b) The agency's proposals for contact, including options for facilitating or achieving any indirect contact or direct contact.	**Update from APR and adoption support plan**
(c) The agency's opinion on the likely effect on the prospective adopter and on the security of the placement of any proposed contact.	**Update from APR**
(d) Where the prospective adopter has been approved by an agency as being suitable to be an adoptive parent, the agency's reasons for considering that the prospective adopter is suitable to be an adoptive parent for this child (with dates of relevant decisions).	**Panel recommendation ADM for match**
Section D: The placement	
(a) Where the child was placed for adoption by an adoption agency (s.18 of the 2002 Act), the date and circumstances of the child's placement with prospective adopter.	
(b) Where the child is living with persons who have applied for the adoption order to be made (s.44 of the 2002 Act), the date when notice of intention to adopt was given.	
(c) Where the placement is being provided with adoption support, this should be summarised and should include the plan and timescales for continuing the support beyond the making of the adoption order.	**Update from adoption support plan**
(d) Where the placement is not being provided with adoption support, the reasons why.	

(e) A summary of the information obtained from the agency's visits and reviews of the placement, including whether the child has been seen separately to the prospective adopter and whether there has been sufficient opportunity to see the family group and the child's interaction in the home environment.	
(f) An assessment of the child's integration within the family of the prospective adopter and the likelihood of the child's full integration into the family and community.	
(g) Any other relevant information that might assist the court.	
Section E: Recommendations	
(a) The relative merits of adoption and other orders with an assessment of whether the child's long-term interests would be best met by an adoption order or by other orders (such as child arrangements or special guardianship orders).	
(b) Recommendations as to whether or not the order sought should be made (and, if not, alternative proposals).	
(c) Recommendations as to whether there should be future contact arrangements (or not).	
Section F: Further information for proceedings relating to Convention adoption orders, Convention adoptions, Section 84 orders or an adoption where Section 83(1) of the 2002 Act applies	
(a) The child's knowledge of their racial and cultural origin.	
(b) The likelihood of the child's adaptation to living in the country he/she is to be placed.	

(c) Where the UK is the State of origin, reasons for considering that, after possibilities for placement of the child within the UK have been given due consideration, intercountry adoption is in the child's best interests.	
(d) Confirmation that the requirements of regulations made under sections 83(4), (5), (6) and (7) and 84(3) and (6) of the 2002 Act have been complied with.	
(e) For a Convention adoption or a Convention adoption order where the UK is either the State of origin or the receiving State, confirmation that the Central Authorities of both States have agreed that the adoption may proceed.	
(f) Where the State of origin is not the UK, the documents supplied by the Central Authority of the State of origin should be attached to the report, together with translation if necessary.	
(g) Where a Convention adoption order is proposed, details of the arrangements which were made for the transfer of the child to the UK and that they were in accordance with the Adoptions with a Foreign Element Regulations 2005 (S.I. 2005/392).	

Appendix 4
Checklist for issues to consider when foster carers are considering adoption

This brief document is a tool to support foster carers and supervising social workers when carers are contemplating adopting the child or children in their care. It is designed to be given to foster carers at an early stage so that they are aware of what will be considered at the point of their Registration of Interest and subsequently in any adoption assessment. It covers the questions that need to be discussed prior to submitting their Registration of Interest and gives a structure for supervising social workers. It is also expected that this will be shared with children's social workers and team managers and Independent Reviewing Officers (IROs) to try and avoid the confusion and difficulty that can ensue in these cases.

1   Adoption is a lifelong commitment

It must be recognised by all parties that there is a fundamental difference between fostering and adoption. Adoption is a legal order that severs ties and possibly relationships with birth family. Legal responsibility for the child is given to the adoptive parent, the local authority retaining little or no involvement. A child cannot be "given back": even if the child and adopters become separated for some reason, parental responsibility remains with the adoptive family. Adoption support may be available but this will very much depend on the child's needs and the perceived needs of the adoptive family. Support will be discussed throughout the assessment and all parties should be clear what this will entail in the particular case in question.

2   Motivation

Carer adopters must be aware that their motivation to adopt this particular child will be explored in great detail and workers must be aware that their views on this will be sought throughout the Stage Two assessment process and the subsequent Adoption Placement Report (Matching Stage). The carer adopters must be advised that all household and close family members will be interviewed as part of the early discussions about the proposed adoption.

3 Health and lifestyle

All prospective adopters have a full medical and their lifestyle is explored in detail. Carer adopters must be advised that they will not be excluded from this process and that full checks and references as well as a medical will be instigated as part of Stage One. Should these enquiries prove problematic, it is possible that the adoption agency may not complete Stage Two.

4 Family situation

The carer adopters must be aware that Stage Two assessment will cover many of the issues already explored in their original fostering assessment, but will require much probing about their capacity to provide permanence for the child in question. They must be advised that their care practices will be explored and evidence taken from their supervision records and annual reviews as well as from the assessing worker.

5 Location and home situation

If the carer adopter does not have physical space for the growing child, then this must be addressed and recognised as a problem. Strategies to overcome this should be discussed prior to accepting any Registration of Interest. The carer must also be advised if the child's social work team and IRO have concerns about the location of the carer adopter's home. Is it too near to that of the birth family? Are there risks attached? Again, the carer must consider these issues at a very early stage.

6 Agency policy and protocols re: fostering after adoption

Carer adopters should be aware from the outset if their fostering service provider, the adoption agency and the child's social worker have any specific views on whether it is appropriate for them to continue fostering if they go on to adopt a particular child in their care.

7 Process

Carer adopters must be advised about timescales, expectations and the agency role and responsibilities.

References

Archer C and Gordon C (2013) *Reparenting the Child Who Hurts*, London: Jessica Kingsley Publishers

ARIS (2014) *Annual Report 2013/2014*, Belfast: ARIS, available at: www.ni-aris.org.uk/sites/default/files/ARIS%20Annual%20Report%202013_2014.pdf

BAAF (2015) *Pupil Premium for Adopted Children: Case studies*, London: BAAF, available at: www.baaf.org.uk/webfm_send/3879

BAAF and Coram (2013) *Fostering for Adoption Practice Guidance*, London: BAAF and Coram, available at: www.baaf.org.uk/webfm_send/3217

Berry M and Barth RP (1990) 'A study of disrupted adoptive placements of adolescents', *Child Welfare*, 69:3, pp 209–225

Biehal N, Ellison S, Baker C and Sinclair I (2010) *Belonging and Permanence: Outcomes in long-term foster care and adoption*, London: BAAF

Borthwick S and Donnelly S (2013) *Concurrent Planning: Achieving early permanence for babies and young children*, London: BAAF

Brodzinsky D (2006) 'Reconceptualising openess in adoption: implications for theory, research and practice', in Brodzinsky D and Palacios J (ed) *Psychological Issues in Adoption: Research and practice*, Westport, CT: Praeger

Burton K (2015) 'The child's health', in Merredew and Sampeys (eds) *Promoting the Health of Children in Public Care*, London: BAAF, pp 13–49

Cairns K (2002) *Attachment, Trauma and Resilience*, London: BAAF

Child Welfare Information Gateway (2013) *Preparing and Supporting Foster Parents Who Adopt*, London: Child Welfare Information Gateway, available at: https://www.childwelfare.gov/pubPDFs/f_fospro.pdf

Conroy Harris A and Bracewell M (2015) 'Consent and legal provision', in Merredew and Sampeys (eds) *Promoting the Health of Children in Public Care*, London: BAAF, pp 89–103

Dance C, Ouwejan D, Beecham J and Farmer E (2010) *Linking and Matching: A survey of adoption agency practice in England and Wales*, London: BAAF

Department for Education (2005) *The Adoption Support Services Regulations 2005*, London: DfE, available at: http://www.legislation.gov.uk/uksi/2005/691/contents/made

Department for Education (2013) *Statutory Guidance on Adoption for Local Authorities, Voluntary Adoption Agencies and Adoption Support Agencies*, London: DfE

Department for Education (2014a) *Statutory Guidance on Adoption for Local Authorities, Voluntary Adoption Agencies and Adoption Support Agencies (Draft)*, London: DfE

Department for Education (2014b) *Statutory Guidance on Adoption for Local Authorities, Voluntary Adoption Agencies and Adoption Support Agencies*, Early permanence placements and approval of prospective adopters as foster carers, London: DfE

Department for Education (2014c) *Court Orders and Pre-Proceedings for Local Authorities*, London: DfE

Dibben E (2013) *Undertaking an Adoption Assessment*, London: BAAF

Fahlberg V (2001) *A Child's Journey Through Placement*, London: BAAF

Gray DD (2012) *Nurturing Adoptions*, London: Jessica Kingsley Publications

Hedley E (2015) 'Health promotion', in Merredew F and Sampeys C (eds) *Promoting the Health of Children in Public Care*, London: BAAF, pp 132–143

Hill M, Lambert L and Triseliotis J (1989) *Achieving Adoption with Love and Money*, London: NCB

Howard J and Smith SL (2003) *After Adoption: The needs of adopted youth*, Washington DC: Child Welfare League of America

Ivaldi G (2000) *Surveying Adoption*, London: BAAF

Kirton D, Beecham J and Ogilvie K (2003) *Remuneration and Performance in Foster Care*, Canterbury: University of Kent

Kirton D, Beecham J and Ogilvie K (2006) 'Adoption by foster carers: a profile of interest and outcomes, *Child and Family Social Work*, 11: 2, pp 139–146

Livingstone Smith S and Donaldson Institute staff (2014) *Facilitating Adoptions from Care*, London: BAAF

McRoy RG (1999) *Special Needs Adoption: Practice note*, New York: Garland Publishing

Merredew F and Sampeys C (ed) (2015) *Promoting the Health of Children in Public Care*, London: BAAF

Neil E, Beek M and Ward E (2015) *Contact after Adoption: A longitudinal study of post-adoption contact arrangements*, London: CoramBAAF

Nicholls EA (2005) *The New Life Work Model*, London: Russell House Publishing

Proch K (1981) 'Foster parents as preferred adoptive parents: practice implications', *Child Welfare*, 60, pp 617–625

Quinton D (2012) *Matching in Adoptions from Care*, London: BAAF

Rowe J, Cain H, Hundleby M and Keane A (1984) *Long-Term Fostering and the Children Act: A study of foster parents who went on to adopt*, London: BAAF

Schofield G and Beek M (2006) *The Attachment Handbook for Foster Care and Adoption*, London: BAAF

Schofield G and Beek M (2014a) *The Secure Base Model: Promoting attachment and resilience in foster care and adoption*, London: BAAF

Schofield G and Beek M (2014b) *Promoting Attachment and Resilience*, London: BAAF

Schofield G and Simmonds J (eds) (2009) *The Child Placement Handbook*, London: BAAF

Scott A and Duncan C (2013) *Understanding Attitudes, Motivations and Barriers to Adoption and Fostering: A marketing proposal for the Department for Education*, London: Kindred

Selwyn J, Meakings S and Wijedasa D (2015) *Beyond the Adoption Order: Challenges, interventions and adoption disruption*, London: BAAF

Selwyn J and Meakings S (2015) *Beyond the Adoption Order (Wales): Discord and disruption in adoptive families*, Bristol: Hadley Centre for Adoption and Foster Care Studies, University of Bristol

Shaw M and Lebens K (1976) 'Children between families', *Adoption & Fostering*, 1:2, pp 17–27

Simmonds J (2014) *The Evidence Base for Matching*, London: BAAF

Sinclair I, Baker C, Wilson K and Gibbs I (2005) *Foster Children: Where they go and how they get on*, London: Jessica Kingsley Publishers

Smith SL and Howard JA (1991) 'A comparative study of successful and disrupted adoptions', *Social Service Review*, 65:2, pp 246–261

Thomas C (2015) *Pupil Premium for Adopted Children: Case studies*, London: BAAF, available at: www.baaf.org.uk/webfm_send/3879

Triseliotis J (2003) 'Long-term foster care or adoption?', in Reder P, Duncan S and Lucey (eds) *Studies in the Assessment of Parenting*, New York: Brunner-Routledge

Vandivere S, Malm K and Radel L (2009) *Adoption USA: A chartbook based on the 2007 National Survey of Adoptive Parents*, Washington DC: US Department of Health and Human Services

Welsh Assembly Government (2007) *Preparing and Assessing Prospective Adopters: Practice guidance*, Cardiff: WAG

Suggested reading for carer adopters

Argent H (2011) *Related by Adoption: A handbook for grandparents and other relatives*, London: BAAF
A short, practical handbook which introduces grandparents-to-be and other relatives to information about adoption. It discusses how the wider family can support the family and adopted child.

Jayne H (2010) *Dale's Tale*, London: BAAF
The story of Helen, a foster carer, and her family, who started looking after Dale as a short-term foster placement but, as the placement became longer than expected, decided to apply to adopt him.

Morrison M (2012) *Talking about Adoption to your Adopted Child*, London: BAAF
A helpful and practical guide which outlines the whys, whens and hows of telling the truth about an adopted child's origins. Includes a chapter dealing specifically with foster carers who adopt fostered children.

Salter A (2012) *The Adopter's Handbook*, London: BAAF
An essential handbook of information for every stage of the adoption process, with advice on health and schooling, helping children with behavioural issues, support for children and adopters, and signposts to useful organisations.

Wolfs R (2008) *Adoption Conversations*, London: BAAF
An in-depth practical guide which explores the questions adopted children are likely to ask, with suggestions for helpful explanations and dialogues.

Wolfs R (2010) *More Adoption Conversations*, London: BAAF
A sequel to *Adoption Conversations*, this guide focuses on the problems that adopted adolescents are likely to confront, with suggestions for helpful solutions and communication methods.